Campbell's®

3 BOOKS IN 1

pil
Publications International, Ltd.

Louis Weber, CEO
Publications International, Ltd.
7373 North Cicero Avenue
Lincolnwood, IL 60712

Pictured on the front cover *(left to right)*: Beef Taco Skillet *(page 97),* Quick Spaghetti & Meatballs *(page 147),* and Slow Cooker Beef & Mushroom Stew *(page 212).*

Pictured on the back cover *(left to right)*: Broccoli & Cheese Casserole *(page 6),* Chicken Noodle & Vegetable Soup *(page 47),* Mushroom-Smothered Beef Burgers *(page 146)*, Slow Cooker Orange Chicken *(page 205)*, and Chicken & Vegetable Bruschetta *(page 240).*

ISBN: 978-1-4508-9778-5

Library of Congress Control Number: 2012942122

Manufactured in China.

8 7 6 5 4 3 2 1

Microwave Cooking: Microwave ovens vary in wattage. Use the cooking times as guidelines and check for doneness before adding more time.

Preparation/Cooking Times: Preparation times are based on the approximate amount of time required to assemble the recipe before cooking, baking, chilling or serving. These times include preparation steps such as measuring, chopping and mixing. The fact that some preparations and cooking can be done simultaneously is taken into account. Preparation of optional ingredients and serving suggestions is not included.

contents

Family-Favorite Casseroles

Sloppy Joe Casserole

Makes 5 servings

PREP TIME
15 minutes

BAKE TIME
15 minutes

- **1 pound ground beef**
- **1 can (10¾ ounces) Campbell's® Condensed Tomato Soup (Regular *or* Healthy Request®)**
- **¼ cup water**
- **1 teaspoon Worcestershire sauce**
- **⅛ teaspoon ground black pepper**
- **1 package (7.5 ounces) refrigerated biscuits (10 biscuits)**
- **½ cup shredded Cheddar cheese (about 2 ounces)**

1. Heat the oven to 400°F.

2. Cook the beef in a 10-inch skillet over medium-high heat until well browned, stirring often to separate the meat. Pour off any fat.

3. Stir the soup, water, Worcestershire and black pepper in the skillet and heat to a boil. Spoon the beef mixture into a 1½-quart casserole. Arrange the biscuits around the inside edge of the casserole.

4. Bake for 15 minutes or until the biscuits are golden brown. Sprinkle the cheese over the beef mixture.

Kitchen Tip

*Sharp **or** mild Cheddar cheese will work in this recipe.*

Broccoli & Cheese Casserole

Makes 6 servings

PREP TIME
10 minutes

BAKE TIME
30 minutes

1 can (10¾ ounces) Campbell's® Condensed Cream of Mushroom Soup (Regular *or* 98% Fat Free)
½ cup milk
2 teaspoons yellow mustard
1 bag (16 ounces) frozen broccoli florets, thawed
1 cup shredded Cheddar cheese (about 4 ounces)
⅓ cup dry bread crumbs
2 teaspoons butter, melted

1. Stir the soup, milk, mustard, broccoli and cheese in a 1½-quart casserole.

2. Stir the bread crumbs and butter in a small bowl. Sprinkle the crumb mixture over the broccoli mixture.

3. Bake at 350°F. for 30 minutes or until the mixture is hot and bubbling.

Rice Is Nice: Add **2 cups** cooked white rice to the broccoli mixture before baking.

Cheese Change-Up: Substitute mozzarella cheese for the Cheddar.

Mexican Lasagna

Makes 8 servings

PREP TIME
30 minutes

BAKE TIME
20 minutes

STAND TIME
5 minutes

Kitchen Tip

***Substitute 1 pound** skinless, boneless chicken breast halves, cut into cubes, for the ground beef.*

- **1 pound ground beef**
- **1 large green pepper, chopped (about 1 cup)**
- **2 cups Prego® Traditional Italian Sauce *or* Tomato Basil & Garlic Italian Sauce**
- **1½ cups Pace® Picante Sauce**
- **1 tablespoon chili powder**
- **8 flour tortillas (6-inch)**
- **2 cups shredded Cheddar cheese (about 8 ounces)**
- **2 cans (2¼ ounces *each*) sliced pitted ripe olives, drained**

1. Heat the oven to 350°F. Cook the beef and pepper in a 10-inch skillet over medium-high heat until beef is well browned, stirring to separate the meat. Pour off any fat.

2. Add the Italian sauce, **1 cup** picante sauce and chili powder. Heat to a boil. Reduce the heat to low and cook for 10 minutes.

3. Spread the remaining picante sauce in a 3-quart shallow baking dish. Arrange **4** tortillas in the dish. Top with **half** of the beef mixture, **half** of the cheese and **half** of the olives. Repeat the layers.

4. Bake for 20 minutes or until the lasagna is hot and bubbling. Let stand for 5 minutes.

Hamburger Pie

Makes 6 servings

- **1½ pounds ground beef**
- **1 can (10¾ ounces) Campbell's® Condensed Cream of Mushroom Soup (Regular *or* 98% Fat Free)**
- **2 packages (8 ounces *each*) refrigerated crescent rolls**
- **1 cup your favorite shredded cheese**

1. Cook the beef in a 10-inch skillet over medium-high heat until well browned, stirring often to separate the meat. Pour off any fat. Stir the soup in the skillet.

2. Unroll **1 package** crescent roll dough and press on the bottom and up the sides of a 9-inch pie plate. Press the seams to seal. Layer **half** the beef mixture and **half** the cheese in the pie plate. Repeat the layers. Unroll the remaining dough. Place the dough over the filling and press the edges to seal, if desired.

3. Bake at 350°F. for 15 minutes or until the crust is golden brown.

PREP TIME
15 minutes

BAKE TIME
15 minutes

Asian Chicken & Rice Bake

Makes 4 servings

PREP TIME
5 minutes

BAKE TIME
45 minutes

- 3/4 cup ***uncooked*** regular long-grain white rice
- 4 skinless, boneless chicken breast halves (about 1 pound)
- 1 can (10 3/4 ounces) Campbell's® Condensed Golden Mushroom Soup
- 3/4 cup water
- 2 tablespoons soy sauce
- 2 tablespoons cider vinegar
- 2 tablespoons honey
- 1 teaspoon garlic powder
- Paprika

1. Spread the rice in a 2-quart shallow baking dish. Top with the chicken.

2. Stir the soup, water, soy sauce, vinegar, honey and garlic powder in a medium bowl. Pour the soup mixture over the chicken. Sprinkle with the paprika. Cover the baking dish.

3. Bake at 375°F. for 45 minutes or until the chicken is cooked through and the rice is tender.

Kitchen Tips

*Add **2 cups** frozen broccoli florets to the rice before baking.*

Sprinkle with toasted sesame seeds after baking.

E-Z Chicken Tortilla Bake

Makes 4 servings

PREP TIME
10 minutes

BAKE TIME
30 minutes

- **1 can (10¾ ounces) Campbell's® Condensed Tomato Soup**
- **1 cup Pace® Picante Sauce**
- **½ cup milk**
- **2 cups cubed cooked chicken**
- **8 corn tortillas (6-inch), cut into 1-inch pieces**
- **1 cup shredded Cheddar cheese (about 4 ounces)**

1. Heat the oven to 400°F. Stir the soup, picante sauce, milk, chicken, tortillas and **half** the cheese in a 2-quart shallow baking dish. Cover the baking dish.

2. Bake for 30 minutes or until chicken mixture is hot and bubbling. Top with the remaining cheese. Let stand until the cheese is melted.

Classic Tuna Noodle Casserole

Makes 4 servings

PREP TIME
10 minutes

BAKE TIME
25 minutes

- **1 can (10¾ ounces) Campbell's® Condensed Cream of Celery Soup (Regular *or* 98% Fat Free)**
- **½ cup milk**
- **1 cup cooked peas**
- **2 tablespoons chopped pimientos**
- **2 cans (about 6 ounces *each*) tuna, drained and flaked**
- **2 cups hot cooked medium egg noodles**
- **2 tablespoons dry bread crumbs**
- **1 tablespoon butter, melted**

1. Heat the oven to 400°F. Stir the soup, milk, peas, pimientos, tuna and noodles in a 1½-quart baking dish. Stir the bread crumbs and butter in a small bowl.

2. Bake for 20 minutes or until the tuna mixture is hot and bubbling. Stir the tuna mixture. Sprinkle with the bread crumb mixture.

3. Bake for 5 minutes or until the bread crumbs are golden brown.

Kitchen Tips

Substitute Campbell's® Condensed Cream of Mushroom Soup for the Cream of Celery.

To melt the butter, remove the wrapper and place the butter in a microwavable cup. Cover and microwave on HIGH for 30 seconds.

Tex-Mex Chicken & Rice Bake

Makes 4 servings

PREP TIME
5 minutes

BAKE TIME
45 minutes

- **1 can (10¾ ounces) Campbell's® Condensed Cream of Chicken Soup (Regular *or* 98% Fat Free)**
- **1 cup Pace® Picante Sauce**
- **½ cup water**
- **1 cup whole kernel corn**
- **¾ cup *uncooked* regular long-grain white rice**
- **4 skinless, boneless chicken breast halves (about 1 pound)**
- **Paprika**
- **½ cup shredded Cheddar cheese (about 2 ounces)**

1. Stir the soup, picante sauce, water, corn and rice in a 2-quart shallow baking dish. Top with the chicken. Sprinkle with the paprika. Cover the baking dish.

2. Bake at 375°F. for 45 minutes or until the chicken is cooked through. Sprinkle with the cheese. Let stand until the cheese is melted.

Cheesy Chicken & Rice Casserole

Makes 4 servings

PREP TIME
15 minutes

BAKE TIME
50 minutes

STAND TIME
10 minutes

- **1 can (10¾ ounces) Campbell's® Condensed Cream of Chicken Soup (Regular, 98% Fat Free *or* Healthy Request®)**
- **1⅓ cups water**
- **¾ cup *uncooked* regular long-grain white rice**
- **½ teaspoon onion powder**
- **¼ teaspoon ground black pepper**
- **2 cups frozen mixed vegetables**
- **4 skinless, boneless chicken breast halves (about 1 pound)**
- **½ cup shredded Cheddar cheese (about 2 ounces)**

1. Heat the oven to 375°F. Stir the soup, water, rice, onion powder, black pepper and vegetables in a 2-quart shallow baking dish.

2. Top with the chicken. Cover the baking dish.

3. Bake for 50 minutes or until the chicken is cooked through and the rice is tender. Top with the cheese. Let the casserole stand for 10 minutes. Stir the rice before serving.

Lower Fat: Use Campbell's® 98% Fat Free Cream of Chicken Soup instead of regular soup and use low-fat cheese instead of regular cheese.

Mexican: In place of the onion powder and black pepper use **1 teaspoon** chili powder. Substitute Mexican cheese blend for the Cheddar.

Italian: In place of the onion powder and black pepper use **1 teaspoon** Italian seasoning, crushed. Substitute ⅓ **cup** shredded Parmesan for the Cheddar.

Kitchen Tip

To Make Alfredo:* *Substitute broccoli florets for the vegetables and substitute* ¼ *cup* *grated Parmesan for the Cheddar cheese.* *Add 2 tablespoons* *Parmesan cheese with the soup. Sprinkle the chicken with the remaining Parmesan cheese.

Cornbread Chicken Pot Pie

Makes 4 servings

- 1 can (10¾ ounces) Campbell's® Condensed Cream of Chicken Soup (Regular *or* 98% Fat Free)
- 1 can (about 8 ounces) whole kernel corn, drained
- 2 cups cubed cooked chicken *or* turkey
- 1 package (about 8 ounces) corn muffin mix
- ¾ cup milk
- 1 egg
- ½ cup shredded Cheddar cheese (about 2 ounces)

1. Heat the oven to 400°F. Stir the soup, corn and chicken in a 9-inch pie plate.

2. Stir the muffin mix, milk and egg in a small bowl just until blended. Spread the batter over the chicken mixture.

3. Bake for 30 minutes or until the topping is golden brown. Sprinkle with the cheese. Let stand until the cheese is melted.

PREP TIME
15 minutes

BAKE TIME
30 minutes

Kitchen Tip

Don't overmix the cornbread batter. Stir just enough to combine the wet ingredients with the dry. Most lumps will disappear during baking.

Turkey Enchiladas

Makes 4 servings

PREP TIME
20 minutes

BAKE TIME
25 minutes

- **1 can (10¾ ounces) Campbell's® Condensed Cream of Celery Soup (Regular *or* 98% Fat Free)**
- **½ cup sour cream**
- **2 tablespoons butter**
- **1 medium onion, chopped (about ½ cup)**
- **1 teaspoon chili powder**
- **2 cups chopped cooked turkey *or* chicken**
- **1 can (about 4 ounces) chopped green chiles**
- **8 flour tortillas (8-inch), warmed**
- **1 cup shredded Cheddar cheese *or* Monterey Jack cheese (about 4 ounces)**

1. Stir the soup and sour cream in a small bowl.

2. Heat the butter in a 3-quart saucepan. Add the onion and chili powder and cook until the onion is tender, stirring occasionally. Stir in the turkey, chiles and **2 tablespoons** soup mixture.

3. Spread **½ cup** soup mixture in a 2-quart shallow baking dish. Spoon **about ¼ cup** turkey mixture down the center of **each** tortilla. Roll up the tortillas and place, seam-side down, into the baking dish. Pour the remaining soup mixture over the filled enchiladas. Sprinkle with the cheese.

4. Bake at 350°F. for 25 minutes or until the enchiladas are hot and bubbling.

Meat Loaf Casserole

Makes 4 servings

PREP TIME
10 minutes

BAKE TIME
20 minutes

- **1 pound ground beef**
- **1 clove garlic, minced**
- **1 can (10¾ ounces) Campbell's® Condensed Vegetable Soup**
- **1 can (10¾ ounces) Campbell's® Condensed Golden Mushroom Soup**
- **1 tablespoon Worcestershire sauce**
- **2 cups water**
- **3 tablespoons butter**
- **¾ cup milk**
- **2 cups instant mashed potato flakes *or* buds**

1. Cook beef and garlic in a 10-inch skillet over medium-high heat until well browned, stirring to separate the meat. Pour off any fat.

2. Stir beef, vegetable soup, ½ **can** mushroom soup and Worcestershire in a 12×8-inch shallow baking dish.

3. Heat remaining soup, water and butter in a 2-quart saucepan over high heat to a boil. Remove from heat. Stir in milk. Slowly stir in potatoes. Spoon potatoes around outer edge of casserole.

4. Bake at 400°F. for 20 minutes or until hot.

All-in-One Meals

Creamy Chicken Florentine

Makes 4 servings

PREP TIME
15 minutes

BAKE TIME
40 minutes

STAND TIME
5 minutes

- **1 can (10¾ ounces) Campbell's® Condensed Cream of Chicken Soup (Regular *or* 98% Fat Free)**
- **1½ cups water**
- **½ of a 20-ounce bag frozen cut leaf spinach, thawed and well drained (about 3½ cups)**
- **1 can (about 14.5 ounces) Italian-style diced tomatoes**
- **1 pound skinless, boneless chicken breasts, cut into 1-inch cubes**
- **2½ cups *uncooked* penne pasta**
- **½ cup shredded mozzarella cheese**

1. Heat the oven to 375°F. Stir the soup, water, spinach, tomatoes and chicken in a 3-quart shallow baking dish. Cover the baking dish.

2. Bake for 20 minutes. Cook the pasta according to the package directions and drain well in a colander. Uncover the baking dish and stir in the pasta.

3. Bake for 20 minutes or until the pasta mixture is hot and bubbling. Sprinkle with the cheese. Let stand for 5 minutes or until the cheese is melted.

Kitchen Tip

Sharp **or** *mild Cheddar cheese will work in this recipe.*

Chicken & Roasted Garlic Risotto

Makes 6 servings

PREP TIME
5 minutes

BAKE TIME
40 minutes

STAND TIME
5 minutes

- **1 can (10¾ ounces) Campbell's® Condensed Cream of Chicken Soup (Regular *or* 98% Fat Free)**
- **1 can (10¾ ounces) Campbell's® Condensed Cream of Mushroom with Roasted Garlic Soup**
- **2 cups water**
- **1 package (10 ounces) frozen peas and carrots (about 2 cups)**
- **1 cup *uncooked* regular long-grain white rice**
- **6 skinless, boneless chicken breast halves (about 1½ pounds)**
- **¼ cup grated Parmesan cheese**

1. Stir the soups, water, vegetables and rice in a 13×9×2-inch (3-quart) shallow baking dish. Top with the chicken. **Cover**.

2. Bake at 375°F. for 40 minutes or until the chicken is cooked through. Sprinkle with the cheese. Let stand for 5 minutes.

Kitchen Tip

Traditionally, risotto is made by sautéing rice in butter then stirring broth into the rice a little at a time—very labor-intensive. This dish gives you the same creamy texture with a lot less work!

Herb Roasted Chicken & Vegetables

Makes 4 servings

- 1 can (10¾ ounces) Campbell's® Condensed Cream of Mushroom Soup (Regular *or* 98% Fat Free)
- ⅓ cup water
- 2 teaspoons dried oregano leaves, crushed
- 4 medium potatoes, cut into quarters (about 1¼ pounds)
- 2 cups fresh *or* frozen baby carrots
- 4 bone-in chicken breast halves (about 2 pounds)
- ½ teaspoon paprika

1. Stir the soup, water, **1 teaspoon** of the oregano, potatoes and carrots in a roasting pan.

2. Top with the chicken. Sprinkle with the remaining oregano and paprika.

3. Bake at 400°F. for 50 minutes or until the chicken is cooked through. Stir the vegetable mixture before serving.

PREP TIME
10 minutes

BAKE TIME
50 minutes

Kitchen Tip

Substitute white wine for the water.

Chicken & Vegetable Bake

Makes 4 servings

PREP TIME
20 minutes

BAKE TIME
30 minutes

- **1 can (10¾ ounces) Campbell's® Condensed Cream of Celery Soup (Regular *or* 98% Fat Free)**
- **½ cup milk**
- **Dash ground black pepper**
- **1 cup cooked broccoli *or* cauliflower florets**
- **1 cup cooked sliced carrots**
- **1 cup cooked cut green beans**
- **¼ cup cooked red pepper strips**
- **1 can (12.5 ounces) Swanson® Premium White Chunk Chicken Breast in Water, drained**
- **1 can (2.8 ounces) French fried onions (1⅓ cups)**

1. Stir the soup, milk, black pepper, broccoli, carrots, green beans, red pepper, chicken and **½ can** onions in a 1½-quart casserole.

2. Bake at 350°F. for 20 minutes or until the chicken mixture is hot and bubbling. Stir the chicken mixture. Sprinkle with the remaining onions.

3. Bake for 10 minutes or until the onions are golden brown.

Easy Chicken Pot Pie

Makes 4 servings

1 can (10¾ ounces) Campbell's® Condensed Cream of Chicken Soup (Regular *or* 98% Fat Free)

1 package (about 9 ounces) frozen mixed vegetables, thawed

1 cup cubed cooked chicken *or* turkey

½ cup milk

1 egg

1 cup all-purpose baking mix

1. Heat the oven to 400°F. Stir the soup, vegetables and chicken in a 9-inch pie plate.

2. Stir the milk, egg and baking mix in a small bowl. Spread the batter over the chicken mixture.

3. Bake for 30 minutes or until the topping is golden brown.

PREP TIME
10 minutes

BAKE TIME
30 minutes

Kitchen Tip

You can easily substitute Campbell's® Condensed Cream of Chicken with Herbs Soup for the Cream of Chicken.

Baked Chicken & Cheese Risotto

Makes 4 servings

PREP TIME
10 minutes

BAKE TIME
45 minutes

STAND TIME
5 minutes

- **1 can (10¾ ounces) Campbell's® Condensed Cream of Mushroom Soup (Regular *or* 98% Fat Free)**
- **1¼ cups water**
- **½ cup milk**
- **¼ cup shredded part-skim mozzarella cheese**
- **3 tablespoons grated Parmesan cheese**
- **1½ cups frozen mixed vegetables**
- **2 skinless, boneless chicken breast halves (about ½ pound), cut into cubes**
- **¾ cup *uncooked* Arborio *or* regular long-grain white rice**

1. Stir the soup, water, milk, mozzarella cheese, Parmesan cheese, vegetables, chicken and rice in a 3-quart shallow baking dish. Cover the baking dish.

2. Bake at 400°F. for 35 minutes. Stir the rice mixture. Cover the baking dish.

3. Bake for 10 minutes or until the chicken is cooked through and the rice is tender. Let stand, covered, for 5 minutes.

Ham Asparagus Gratin

Makes 4 servings

PREP TIME
20 minutes

BAKE TIME
30 minutes

- **1 can (10¾ ounces) Campbell's® Condensed Cream of Asparagus Soup**
- **½ cup milk**
- **¼ teaspoon onion powder**
- **¼ teaspoon ground black pepper**
- **1½ cups cooked cut asparagus**
- **1½ cups cubed cooked ham**
- **2¼ cups corkscrew-shaped pasta (rotini), cooked and drained**
- **1 cup shredded Cheddar cheese *or* Swiss cheese**

1. Stir the soup, milk, onion powder, black pepper, asparagus, ham, pasta and **½ cup** cheese in a 2-quart shallow baking dish.

2. Bake at 400°F. for 25 minutes or until the ham mixture is hot and bubbling. Stir the ham mixture. Sprinkle with the remaining cheese.

3. Bake for 5 minutes or until the cheese is melted.

Zucchini, Chicken & Rice Casserole

Makes 4 servings

PREP TIME
15 minutes

BAKE TIME
35 minutes

STAND TIME
10 minutes

Vegetable cooking spray
- **1 package (12 ounces) refrigerated *or* thawed frozen breaded cooked chicken tenders, cut into bite-sized strips**
- **2 large zucchini, cut in half lengthwise and thinly sliced (about 4 cups)**
- **1 jar (7 ounces) whole roasted sweet peppers, drained and thinly sliced**
- **1 cup *uncooked* quick-cooking brown rice**
- **1 can (10¾ ounces) Campbell's® Condensed Cream of Celery Soup (Regular *or* 98% Fat Free)**
- **1 soup can water**
- **½ cup sour cream**

1. Heat the oven to 375°F. Spray a 3-quart shallow baking dish with the cooking spray.

2. Stir the chicken, zucchini, peppers and rice in the baking dish.

3. Stir the soup, water and sour cream in a small bowl. Pour the soup mixture over the chicken mixture. Cover the baking dish.

4. Bake for 35 minutes or until the rice is tender. Let stand for 10 minutes. Stir the rice before serving.

Kitchen Tip

Choose zucchini that have firm, dark green skin.

Turkey and Stuffing Casserole

Makes 6 servings

PREP TIME
15 minutes

BAKE TIME
25 minutes

- **Vegetable cooking spray**
- **1 can (10¾ ounces) Campbell's® Condensed Cream of Mushroom Soup (Regular *or* 98% Fat Free)**
- **1 cup milk *or* water**
- **1 bag (16 ounces) frozen vegetable combination (broccoli, cauliflower, carrots), thawed**
- **2 cups cubed cooked turkey *or* chicken**
- **4 cups Pepperidge Farm® Herb Seasoned Stuffing**
- **1 cup shredded Swiss *or* Cheddar cheese (about 4 ounces)**

1. Heat the oven to 400°F. Spray a 2-quart casserole with the cooking spray.

2. Stir the soup and milk in a large bowl. Add the vegetables, turkey and stuffing and mix lightly. Spoon the turkey mixture into the casserole.

3. Bake for 20 minutes or until the turkey mixture is hot and bubbling. Stir the turkey mixture. Top with the cheese.

4. Bake for 5 minutes or until the cheese is melted.

Kitchen Tip

Substitute 3 cans (4.5 ounces each) Swanson® Premium White Chunk Chicken Breast in Water, drained, for the cubed cooked turkey.

Easy Chicken & Biscuits

Makes 4 servings

PREP TIME
10 minutes

BAKE TIME
35 minutes

- 1 can (10¾ ounces) Campbell's® Condensed Cream of Broccoli Soup (Regular *or* 98% Fat Free)
- 1 can (10¾ ounces) Campbell's® Condensed Cream of Potato Soup
- ⅔ cup milk
- ½ teaspoon poultry seasoning
- ⅛ teaspoon ground black pepper
- 2 cups frozen mixed vegetables
- 2 cups cubed cooked chicken *or* turkey
- 1 package (7.5 ounces) refrigerated biscuits

1. Stir the soups, milk, poultry seasoning, black pepper, vegetables and chicken in a 2-quart shallow baking dish.

2. Bake at 400°F. for 20 minutes or until the chicken mixture is hot and bubbling. Stir the chicken mixture. Top with the biscuits.

3. Bake for 15 minutes or until the biscuits are golden brown.

Kitchen Tip

Substitute Campbell's® Condensed Cream of Celery Soup for the Cream of Broccoli.

Chicken Broccoli Divan

Makes 4 servings

PREP TIME
15 minutes

BAKE TIME
20 minutes

- **1 pound fresh broccoli, cut into spears *or* 1 package (10 ounces) frozen broccoli spears, cooked and drained**
- **1 can (12.5 ounces) Swanson® Premium White Chunk Chicken Breast in Water, drained**
- **1 can (10¾ ounces) Campbell's® Condensed Broccoli Cheese Soup (Regular *or* 98% Fat Free)**
- **⅓ cup milk**
- **½ cup shredded Cheddar cheese**
- **2 tablespoons dry bread crumbs**
- **1 tablespoon butter, melted**

1. Place the broccoli and chicken into a 9-inch pie plate. Stir the soup and milk in a small bowl. Pour the soup mixture over the broccoli and chicken.

2. Sprinkle the cheese over the soup mixture. Stir the bread crumbs and butter in a small bowl. Sprinkle the bread crumb mixture over the cheese.

3. Bake at 450°F. for 20 minutes or until the cheese is melted and the bread crumb mixture is golden brown.

Kitchen Tip

For cornflake topping, substitute cornflakes for the bread crumbs and omit the butter.

Broccoli Fish Bake

Makes 4 servings

PREP TIME
15 minutes

BAKE TIME
20 minutes

1 **package (about 10 ounces) frozen broccoli spears, cooked and drained**

4 **fresh *or* thawed frozen firm white fish fillets (cod, haddock *or* halibut) (about 1 pound)**

1 **can (10¾ ounces) Campbell's® Condensed Cream of Broccoli Soup**

⅓ **cup milk**

¼ **cup shredded Cheddar cheese**

2 **tablespoons dry bread crumbs**

1 **teaspoon butter, melted**

⅛ **teaspoon paprika**

1. Place the broccoli into a 2-quart shallow baking dish. Top with the fish. Stir the soup and milk in a small bowl. Pour the soup mixture over the fish. Sprinkle with the cheese.

2. Stir the bread crumbs, butter and paprika in a small bowl. Sprinkle the crumb mixture over all.

3. Bake at 450°F. for 20 minutes or until the fish flakes easily when tested with a fork.

Kitchen Tip

You can substitute 1 pound fresh broccoli spears, cooked and drained, for the frozen.

Country Turkey Casserole

Makes 5 servings

1 can (10¾ ounces) Campbell's® Condensed Cream of Celery Soup (Regular *or* 98% Fat Free)

1 can (10¾ ounces) Campbell's® Condensed Cream of Potato Soup

1 cup milk

¼ teaspoon dried thyme leaves, crushed

⅛ teaspoon ground black pepper

4 cups cooked cut-up vegetables*

2 cups cubed cooked turkey *or* chicken

4 cups prepared Pepperidge Farm® Herb Seasoned Stuffing

Use a combination of cut green beans **and sliced carrots.*

1. Stir the soups, milk, thyme, black pepper, vegetables and turkey in a 3-quart shallow baking dish. Spoon the stuffing over the turkey mixture.

2. Bake at 400°F. for 25 minutes or until the stuffing is golden brown.

PREP TIME
10 minutes

BAKE TIME
25 minutes

Soups, Stews & Chilis

Mediterranean Fish Soup

Makes 6 servings

PREP TIME
10 minutes

COOK TIME
20 minutes

- **2 tablespoons olive oil**
- **1 large sweet onion, chopped (about 2 cups)**
- **¼ cup dry white wine *or* Swanson® Chicken Broth**
- **4 cups Swanson® Vegetable Broth *or* Chicken Broth (Regular *or* Certified Organic)**
- **1 can (14.5 ounces) diced tomatoes, undrained**
- **24 mussels, scrubbed and beards removed**
- **1 pound firm white fish fillet (cod, haddock *or* halibut), cut into 1-inch pieces**
- **½ pound fresh *or* thawed frozen large shrimp, peeled and deveined**
- **Shredded fresh basil leaves**

1. Heat the oil in a 6-quart saucepot over medium heat. Add the onion and cook until tender.

2. Add the wine and cook for 1 minute. Stir in the broth and tomatoes and heat to a boil. Reduce the heat to low. Add the mussels, fish and shrimp. Cover and cook until the mussels open, the fish flakes easily when tested with a fork and the shrimp are cooked through. Discard any mussels that do not open. Season as desired. Garnish with the basil.

Kitchen Tip

Select mussels with tightly closed shells or shells that snap shut when lightly tapped. Avoid mussels with broken shells.

West African Vegetable Stew

Makes 6 servings

PREP TIME
15 minutes

COOK TIME
30 minutes

1 tablespoon vegetable oil
2 large onions, sliced (about 2 cups)
2 cloves garlic, minced
1 pound sweet potatoes, peeled, cut in half lengthwise and cut into ¼-inch slices
1 large tomato, coarsely chopped (about 2 cups)
½ cup raisins
½ teaspoon ground cinnamon
½ teaspoon crushed red pepper
1 can (10½ ounces) Campbell's® Condensed Chicken Broth
½ cup water
1 can (about 15 ounces) chickpeas (garbanzo beans), rinsed and drained
4 coarsely chopped fresh spinach leaves
Hot cooked rice *or* couscous

1. Heat the oil in a 12-inch skillet over medium heat. Add the onion and garlic and cook until the onion is tender.

2. Add the potatoes and tomato to the skillet and cook for 5 minutes. Stir in the raisins, cinnamon, red pepper, broth and water and heat to a boil. Reduce the heat to low. Cover and cook for 15 minutes or until the potatoes are tender.

3. Stir in the chickpeas and spinach and cook until the spinach is wilted. Serve with the rice, if desired.

Chili & Rice

Makes 4 servings

- ¾ pound ground beef (85% lean)
- 1 medium onion, chopped (about ½ cup)
- 1 tablespoon chili powder
- 1 can (10¾ ounces) Campbell's® Healthy Request® Condensed Tomato Soup
- ¼ cup water
- 1 teaspoon vinegar
- 1 can (about 15 ounces) kidney beans, rinsed and drained
- 4 cups hot cooked regular long-grain white rice, cooked without salt

1. Cook the beef, onion and chili powder in a 10-inch skillet over medium-high heat until the beef is well browned, stirring often. Pour off any fat.

2. Stir the soup, water, vinegar and beans in the skillet and heat to a boil. Reduce the heat to low. Cook for 10 minutes or until the mixture is hot and bubbling. Serve the beef mixture over the rice.

PREP TIME
10 minutes

COOK TIME
25 minutes

Kitchen Tip

This dish is delicious served topped with shredded reduced-fat Cheddar cheese.

French Onion Soup

Makes 4 servings

PREP TIME
10 minutes

COOK TIME
45 minutes

- **1 tablespoon vegetable oil**
- **2½ large onions, halved and thinly sliced (about 2½ cups)***
- **¼ teaspoon sugar**
- **2 tablespoons all-purpose flour**
- **3½ cups Swanson® Beef Broth (Regular, Lower Sodium *or* Certified Organic)**
- **¼ cup dry white wine *or* vermouth**
- **4 slices French bread, toasted****
- **½ cup shredded Swiss cheese**

****Use a food processor with slicing attachment for ease in preparation.***

*****For even more flavor, try rubbing the bread with a garlic clove and topping it with the cheese before toasting.***

1. Heat the oil in a 4-quart saucepot over medium heat. Add the onions. Reduce the heat to low. Cover and cook for 15 minutes. Uncover the saucepot.

2. Increase the heat to medium. Add the sugar and cook for 15 minutes or until the onions are golden.

3. Stir the flour in the saucepot and cook and stir for 1 minute. Stir in the broth and wine. Heat to a boil. Reduce the heat to low. Cook for 10 minutes.

4. Divide the soup among **4** bowls. Top **each** with a bread slice and cheese.

Chicken Corn Chowder

Makes 4 servings

PREP TIME
10 minutes

COOK TIME
5 minutes

- **1 can (10¾ ounces) Campbell's® Condensed Cream of Celery Soup (Regular *or* 98% Fat Free)**
- **1 soup can milk**
- **½ cup Pace® Picante Sauce**
- **1 can (about 8 ounces) whole kernel corn, drained**
- **1 cup cubed cooked chicken *or* turkey**
- **4 slices bacon, cooked and crumbled**
- **Shredded Cheddar cheese**
- **Sliced green onion**

1. Heat the soup, milk, picante sauce, corn, chicken and bacon in a 3-quart saucepan over medium heat until the mixture is hot and bubbling, stirring occasionally.

2. Sprinkle with the cheese and onion. Drizzle **each** serving with additional picante sauce.

Kitchen Tip

Substitute Campbell's® Condensed Cream of Chicken Soup for the Cream of Celery.

Beef and Brew Stew

Makes 8 servings

PREP TIME
20 minutes

COOK TIME
40 minutes

BAKE TIME
2 hours

- **3 tablespoons vegetable oil**
- **3 pounds boneless beef chuck roasts, cut into 1-inch pieces**
- **2 large onions, sliced (about 2 cups)**
- **2 cloves garlic, minced**
- **2 cans (10¾ ounces *each*) Campbell's® Condensed Golden Mushroom Soup**
- **2 cans (10½ ounces *each*) Campbell's® Condensed French Onion Soup**
- **1 bottle (12 fluid ounces) dark beer *or* stout**
- **1 tablespoon packed brown sugar**
- **1 tablespoon cider vinegar**
- **½ teaspoon dried thyme leaves, crushed**
- **1 bay leaf**
- **2 cups fresh *or* frozen whole baby carrots**
- **Egg noodles, cooked, drained and buttered**

1. Heat **1 tablespoon oil** in an oven-safe 6-quart saucepot over medium-high heat. Add the beef in 3 batches and cook until well browned, stirring often, adding an additional **1 tablespoon** oil as needed during cooking. Remove the beef from the saucepot. Pour off any fat.

2. Heat the remaining oil in the saucepot over medium heat. Add the onions and garlic and cook until the onions are tender.

3. Stir the soups, beer, brown sugar, vinegar, thyme, bay leaf and carrots in the saucepot and heat to a boil. Cover the saucepot.

4. Bake at 300°F. for 2 hours or until the beef is fork-tender. Discard the bay leaf. Serve the beef mixture over the noodles.

Southwest White Chicken Chili

Makes 6 servings

PREP TIME
10 minutes

COOK TIME
20 minutes

- **1 tablespoon vegetable oil**
- **4 skinless, boneless chicken breast halves (about 1 pound), cut into cubes**
- **4 teaspoons chili powder**
- **2 teaspoons ground cumin**
- **1 large onion, chopped (about 1 cup)**
- **1 medium green pepper, chopped (about ¾ cup)**
- **1 can (10¾ ounces) Campbell's® Condensed Cream of Chicken Soup (Regular *or* 98% Fat Free)**
- **¾ cup water**
- **1½ cups frozen whole kernel corn**
- **2 cans (about 15 ounces *each*) white kidney beans (cannellini), rinsed and drained**
- **2 tablespoons shredded Cheddar cheese**

1. Heat the oil in a 4-quart saucepan over medium-high heat. Add the chicken, chili powder, cumin, onion and pepper and cook until the chicken is cooked through and the vegetables are tender, stirring often.

2. Stir the soup, water, corn and beans in the saucepan and heat to a boil. Reduce the heat to low. Cover and cook for 5 minutes, stirring occasionally. Sprinkle with the cheese.

Hearty Vegetarian Chili

Makes 4 servings

- **2 tablespoons vegetable oil**
- **1 large onion, chopped (about 1 cup)**
- **1 small green pepper, chopped (about ½ cup)**
- **¼ teaspoon garlic powder *or* 2 small garlic cloves, minced**
- **1 tablespoon chili powder**
- **½ teaspoon ground cumin**
- **2½ cups V8® 100% Vegetable Juice**
- **1 can (about 15 ounces) black beans *or* red kidney beans, rinsed and drained**
- **1 can (about 15 ounces) pinto beans, rinsed and drained**

1. Heat the oil in a 2-quart saucepan over medium heat. Add the onion, green pepper, garlic powder, chili powder and cumin and cook until the vegetables are tender, stirring occasionally.

2. Stir the vegetable juice in the saucepan and heat to a boil. Reduce the heat to low. Cook for 5 minutes.

3. Stir in the beans and cook until the mixture is hot and bubbling.

PREP TIME
10 minutes

COOK TIME
20 minutes

Spicy Mexican Minestrone Stew

Makes 6 servings

PREP TIME
15 minutes

COOK TIME
35 minutes

- **½ pound sweet Italian pork sausage, casing removed**
- **2 teaspoons vegetable oil**
- **1¾ cups Swanson® Beef Stock**
- **1 can (14.5 ounces) whole peeled tomatoes, cut up**
- **1½ cups Pace® Picante Sauce**
- **¼ teaspoon garlic powder *or* 1 clove garlic, minced**
- **1 cup *uncooked* medium shell-shaped pasta**
- **1 package (about 10 ounces) frozen cut green beans, thawed (about 2 cups)**
- **1 can (about 15 ounces) kidney beans, rinsed and drained**
- **Shredded Monterey Jack cheese *or* mozzarella cheese**

1. Shape the sausage firmly into ½-inch meatballs.

2. Heat the oil in a 4-quart saucepan over medium-high heat. Add the meatballs and cook until they're well browned. Remove the meatballs from the saucepan. Pour off any fat.

3. Add the stock, tomatoes, picante sauce and garlic powder to the saucepan and heat to a boil. Stir in the pasta. Return the meatballs to the saucepan. Reduce the heat to low. Cover and cook for 10 minutes, stirring often.

4. Stir in the green beans and kidney beans. Cook for 10 minutes or until the meatballs are cooked through and the pasta is tender, stirring occasionally. Sprinkle with the cheese before serving, if desired.

Kitchen Tips

Substitute 1 can (about 16 ounces) cut green beans, drained for the frozen. For quicker preparation, omit the first step and cook the sausage over medium-high heat until well browned, stirring often to separate the meat. Leave the sausage in the skillet and pour off any fat. Proceed with the remainder of the recipe as directed.

Creamy Southwest Tomato Soup

Makes 6 servings

2 cans (10¾ ounces *each*) Campbell's® Condensed Tomato Soup

2 soup cans milk

1 jar (16 ounces) Pace® Picante Sauce

Heat the soup, milk and picante sauce in a 3-quart saucepan over medium heat until the mixture is hot and bubbling.

PREP TIME
5 minutes

COOK TIME
5 minutes

Chicken Soup with Matzo Balls

Makes 6 servings

PREP TIME
20 minutes

CHILL TIME
2 hours

COOK TIME
45 minutes

Kitchen Tip

To keep the matzo balls light and fluffy, remember not to lift the lid during the first 30 to 35 minutes of cooking.

- **4 large eggs**
- **¼ cup olive oil**
- **10 cups Swanson® Natural Goodness® Chicken Broth**
- **1 cup matzo meal**
- **3 tablespoons chopped fresh dill weed *or* parsley *or* ⅛ teaspoon ground ginger (optional)**

1. Stir the eggs and the olive oil in a large bowl with a whisk until foamy. Stir in **3 tablespoons** of the broth. Stir in the matzo meal and any of the optional seasonings. Cover the bowl and refrigerate for 2 hours.

2. Heat **4 quarts** of water in a 6-quart saucepot over high heat to a boil. Shape the batter into 1-inch balls. Stir the matzo balls into the boiling water. Reduce the heat to low. Cover the saucepot and cook for 35 to 45 minutes or until they're cooked through. Remove the matzo balls from the saucepot and set them aside.

3. Heat the **remaining** broth in a 6-quart saucepot over medium-high heat to a boil. Stir the matzo balls in the saucepot. Reduce the heat to low and cook until they're heated through. Serve in **6** shallow bowls.

Southwestern Black Bean Soup

Makes 4 servings

1 can (10¼ ounces) Campbell's® Beef Gravy

3 cans (about 15 ounces *each*) black beans, rinsed and drained

1 cup V8® 100% Vegetable Juice

½ cup Pace® Picante Sauce

1 teaspoon ground cumin

¼ cup sour cream

¼ cup shredded Cheddar cheese

1. Place the gravy and **1 can** beans into a blender. Cover and blend until the mixture is smooth. Pour the gravy mixture into a 3-quart saucepan.

2. Stir the remaining beans, vegetable juice, picante sauce and cumin in the saucepan and heat to a boil. Reduce the heat to low. Cover and cook for 5 minutes. Serve with the sour cream and cheese.

PREP TIME
5 minutes

COOK TIME
10 minutes

Shortcut Beef Stew

Makes 4 servings

PREP TIME
5 minutes

COOK TIME
25 minutes

- **1 tablespoon vegetable oil**
- **1 boneless beef sirloin steak, ¾-inch thick (about 1 pound), cut into 1-inch pieces**
- **1 can (10¾ ounces) Campbell's® Condensed Tomato Soup**
- **1 can (10½ ounces) Campbell's® Condensed French Onion Soup**
- **1 tablespoon Worcestershire sauce**
- **1 bag (24 ounces) frozen vegetables for stew (potatoes, carrots, celery)**

1. Heat the oil in a 10-inch skillet over medium-high heat. Add the beef and cook until well browned, stirring often. Pour off any fat.

2. Stir the soups, Worcestershire and vegetables in the skillet and heat to a boil. Reduce the heat to low. Cover and cook for 10 minutes or until the beef is cooked through and the vegetables are tender.

Kitchen Tips

Substitute 5 cups frozen vegetables (carrots, small whole onions, cut green beans, cauliflower, zucchini, peas or lima beans) for the frozen vegetables for stew.

Substitute Campbell's® Condensed Beefy Mushroom Soup for the French Onion Soup.

Chicken Noodle & Vegetable Soup

Makes 6 servings

6 cups Swanson® Chicken Broth (Regular, Natural Goodness® *or* Certified Organic)
1 teaspoon onion powder
½ teaspoon dried basil leaves, crushed
¼ teaspoon garlic powder
1 package (about 9 ounces) frozen mixed vegetables
1 cup *uncooked* medium egg noodles

Stir the broth, onion powder, basil, garlic powder and vegetables in a 3-quart saucepan. Heat to a boil over medium-high heat. Stir in the noodles. Cook for 5 minutes or until the noodles are done.

PREP TIME
5 minutes

COOK TIME
20 minutes

Italian Wedding Soup

Makes 10 servings

PREP TIME
15 minutes

COOK TIME
25 minutes

- 1 pound lean ground beef
- 1 egg ***or*** 2 egg whites
- ½ cup fresh bread crumbs
- 3 tablespoons grated Parmesan cheese
- 2 tablespoons grated onions
- ¼ teaspoon ground black pepper
- 12 cups Swanson® Chicken Broth (Regular, Natural Goodness® ***or*** Certified Organic)
- 1 teaspoon onion powder
- 1 teaspoon garlic powder
- 1 teaspoon celery salt
- ⅔ cup orzo pasta (rice-shaped pasta)
- 2 cups thinly sliced escarole
- Grated Parmesan cheese

1. Mix **thoroughly** the beef, egg, bread crumbs, cheese, onions and pepper. Shape **firmly** into ½-inch balls.

2. Heat the broth, onion powder, garlic powder and celery salt in a 6-quart saucepot over medium-high heat to a boil. Stir the meatballs into the saucepot. Reduce the heat to low and cook for 10 minutes or until they're cooked through. Remove the meatballs and set them aside.

3. Stir the orzo in the saucepot and cook for 5 minutes. Stir the escarole in the saucepot. Return the meatballs to the saucepot and cook until they're heated through. Sprinkle with the cheese.

Kitchen Tip

The secret to this recipe's flavor is the cheese, add a tablespoon or two to the finished soup to enhance the flavor!

Country Chicken Soup

Makes 4 servings

- 5¼ cups Swanson® Chicken Broth (Regular, Natural Goodness® *or* Certified Organic)
- ⅛ teaspoon poultry seasoning
- ⅛ teaspoon dried thyme leaves, crushed
- 1 medium carrot, sliced (about ½ cup)
- 1 stalk celery, sliced (about ½ cup)
- 1 small onion, finely chopped (about ¼ cup)
- ½ cup ***uncooked*** regular long-grain white rice
- 2 cans (4.5 ounces ***each***) Swanson® Premium White Chunk Chicken Breast in Water, drained

1. Stir the broth, poultry seasoning, thyme, carrot, celery and onion in a 3-quart saucepan. Over medium-high heat, heat to a boil. Stir in the rice. Reduce the heat to low.

2. Cover the saucepan and cook for 20 minutes or until the rice is done.

3. Stir the chicken in the saucepan and heat through.

PREP TIME
10 minutes

COOK TIME
30 minutes

Asian Chicken Noodle Soup

Makes 4 servings

PREP TIME
5 minutes

COOK TIME
20 minutes

3½ cups Swanson® Chicken Broth (Regular, Natural Goodness® *or* Certified Organic)
1 teaspoon soy sauce
1 teaspoon ground ginger
Generous dash ground black pepper
1 medium carrot, diagonally sliced
1 stalk celery, diagonally sliced
½ red pepper, cut into 2-inch-long strips
2 green onions, diagonally sliced
1 clove garlic, minced
½ cup broken-up *uncooked* curly Asian noodles
1 cup shredded cooked chicken

1. Heat the broth, soy sauce, ginger, black pepper, carrot, celery, red pepper, green onions and garlic in a 2-quart saucepan over medium-high heat to a boil.

2. Stir the noodles and chicken in the saucepan. Reduce the heat to medium and cook for 10 minutes or until the noodles are done.

Kitchen Tip

***For an Interesting Twist:** Use 1 cup sliced bok choy for the celery and 2 ounces uncooked cellophane noodles for the curly Asian noodles. Reduce the cook time to 5 minutes.*

Savory Vegetable Beef Soup

Makes 6 servings

- **1¾ cups Swanson® Beef Broth (Regular, Lower Sodium *or* Certified Organic)**
- **2 medium potatoes, cut into cubes**
- **1 cup cubed cooked beef**
- **3 cups V8® 100% Vegetable Juice**
- **1 can (about 8 ounces) whole peeled tomatoes, cut up**
- **1 bag (16 ounces) frozen mixed vegetables**
- **¼ teaspoon dried thyme leaves, crushed**
- **⅛ teaspoon ground black pepper**

1. Place the broth and potatoes in a 4-quart saucepan and heat to a boil over medium-high heat. Reduce the heat to low. Cover and cook for 5 minutes or until the potatoes are tender.

2. Stir the beef, vegetable juice, tomatoes, vegetables, thyme and black pepper in the saucepan. Cover and cook for 15 minutes or until the vegetables are tender.

PREP TIME
10 minutes

COOK TIME
20 minutes

Moroccan Chicken Stew

Makes 4 servings

PREP TIME
10 minutes

COOK TIME
40 minutes

- **2 tablespoons olive oil**
- **8 skinless, bone-in chicken thighs (about 2 pounds)**
- **2 medium red onions, sliced (about 2 cups)**
- **1 large green pepper, cut into 1-inch pieces (about 1½ cups)**
- **2 cloves garlic, finely chopped**
- **1 teaspoon ground cinnamon**
- **1 tablespoon curry powder**
- **1 can (10¾ ounces) Campbell's® Condensed Tomato Soup**
- **⅓ cup golden raisins**
- **1 can (about 15 ounces) chickpeas (garbanzo beans), rinsed and drained**
- **⅓ cup slivered almonds, toasted**

1. Heat the oil in a 5-quart saucepot over medium-high heat. Add the chicken in batches and cook until well browned on both sides. Remove the chicken from the saucepot.

2. Reduce the heat to medium. Add the onions, green pepper and garlic and cook for 5 minutes or until tender-crisp. Add the cinnamon and curry and cook and stir for 1 minute. Stir in the soup and heat to a boil. Return the chicken to the saucepot. Reduce the heat to low. Cover and cook for 15 minutes.

3. Stir the raisins and chickpeas in the saucepot. Cook for 10 minutes or until the chicken is cooked through. Stir in the almonds.

South-of-the-Border Beef Stew

Makes 6 servings

PREP TIME
10 minutes

COOK TIME
30 minutes

- **1½ pounds ground beef**
- **1 large onion, chopped (about 1 cup)**
- **½ teaspoon garlic powder *or* 2 cloves garlic, minced**
- **1 can (10¾ ounces) Campbell's® Condensed Tomato Soup**
- **1 can (10½ ounces) Campbell's® Condensed Beef Broth**
- **1 cup water**
- **2 tablespoons chili powder**
- **3 medium potatoes, cut into cubes (about 3 cups)**
- **1 can (about 16 ounces) whole kernel corn, drained**
- **Shredded Cheddar cheese**

1. Cook the beef, onion and garlic powder in a 12-inch skillet over medium-high heat until the beef is well browned, stirring often to separate the meat. Pour off any fat.

2. Stir the soup, broth, water, chili powder and potatoes in the skillet and heat to a boil. Reduce the heat to low. Cover and cook for 15 minutes or until the potatoes are tender. Stir in the corn and cook until the mixture is hot and bubbling. Sprinkle with the cheese.

Chicken Tortilla Soup

Makes 4 servings

PREP TIME
15 minutes

BAKE TIME
15 minutes

COOK TIME
10 minutes

Kitchen Tip

For 1½ cups chopped cooked chicken, heat 4 cups water in a 2-quart saucepan over medium heat to a boil. Add ¾ pound skinless boneless chicken breast halves or thighs, cut into cubes, and cook for 5 minutes or until the chicken is cooked through. Drain the chicken well in a colander.

4 corn tortillas (6-inch), cut into strips
3½ cups Swanson® Chicken Broth (Regular, Natural Goodness® *or* Certified Organic)
½ cup Pace® Picante Sauce
1 teaspoon garlic powder
1 can (14.5 ounces) whole peeled tomatoes, cut up
2 medium carrots, shredded (about 1 cup)
1½ cups chopped cooked chicken

1. Heat the oven to 400°F. Place the tortilla strips on a baking sheet.

2. Bake for 15 minutes or until they're golden.

3. Heat the broth, picante sauce, garlic powder, tomatoes and carrots in a 2-quart saucepan over medium-high heat to a boil. Reduce the heat to low. Cook for 5 minutes.

4. Stir the chicken in the saucepan and cook until the mixture is hot and bubbling. Top with the tortilla strips before serving.

Southwestern Chicken Chili

Makes 6 servings

2 tablespoons olive oil
1 cup chopped onion
½ cup chopped celery
½ cup chopped red pepper
3 tablespoons all-purpose flour
1 tablespoon ground cumin
2 cups Swanson® Chicken Stock
2 cans (15 ounces *each*) great Northern beans
1 jar (16 ounces) Pace® Picante Sauce
2 cups chopped cooked chicken
Shredded Pepper Jack cheese
Cubed avocado

1. Heat the oil in a 4-quart saucepot over medium heat. Add the onion, celery and red pepper and cook until tender. Stir in the flour and cumin and cook for 2 minutes. Stir the stock in the saucepot. Cook and stir until the mixture boils.

2. Stir the beans, picante sauce and chicken in the saucepot. Heat to a boil. Reduce the heat to low. Cook for 20 minutes.

3. Garnish with the cheese and avocado.

PREP TIME
15 minutes

COOK TIME
35 minutes

Oodles of Noodles

Three Cheese Baked Ziti with Spinach

Makes 6 servings

PREP TIME
15 minutes

BAKE TIME
30 minutes

- **1 package (16 ounces) *uncooked* medium tube-shaped pasta (ziti)**
- **1 bag (6 ounces) baby spinach, washed (about 4 cups)**
- **1 jar (1 pound 9 ounces) Prego® Marinara Italian Sauce**
- **1 cup ricotta cheese**
- **4 ounces shredded mozzarella cheese (about 1 cup)**
- **¾ cup grated Parmesan cheese**
- **½ teaspoon garlic powder**
- **¼ teaspoon ground black pepper**

1. Prepare the pasta according to the package directions. Add the spinach during the last minute of the cooking time. Drain the pasta and spinach well in a colander. Return them to the saucepot.

2. Stir the Italian sauce, ricotta, **½ cup** of the mozzarella cheese, **½ cup** of the Parmesan cheese, garlic powder and black pepper into the pasta mixture. Spoon the pasta mixture into a 13×9×2-inch shallow baking dish. Sprinkle with the remaining mozzarella and Parmesan cheeses.

3. Bake at 350°F. for 30 minutes or until the mixture is hot and bubbling.

Chicken Florentine Lasagna

Makes 6 servings

PREP TIME
10 minutes

BAKE TIME
1 hour

STAND TIME
10 minutes

Kitchen Tip

To thaw the spinach, microwave on HIGH for 3 minutes, breaking the spinach apart with a fork halfway through heating.

2 cans (10¾ ounces *each*) Campbell's® Condensed Cream of Chicken with Herbs Soup
2 cups milk
1 egg
1 container (15 ounces) ricotta cheese
6 *uncooked* lasagna noodles
1 package (about 10 ounces) frozen chopped spinach, thawed and well drained
2 cups cubed cooked chicken *or* turkey
2 cups shredded Cheddar cheese (about 8 ounces)

1. Stir the soup and milk in a small bowl until smooth. Stir the egg and ricotta in a medium bowl.

2. Spread **1 cup** soup mixture in a 3-quart shallow baking dish. Top with **3 uncooked** lasagna noodles, ricotta mixture, spinach, chicken, **1 cup** Cheddar cheese and **1 cup** soup mixture. Top with remaining **uncooked** lasagna noodles and remaining soup mixture. Cover the baking dish.

3. Bake at 375°F. for 1 hour or until the lasagna is hot. Uncover the baking dish. Top with the remaining Cheddar cheese. Let stand for 10 minutes.

Cheddar Penne with Sausage & Peppers

Makes 6 servings

PREP TIME
20 minutes

COOK TIME
20 minutes

- **1 tablespoon olive oil**
- **1 pound sweet Italian pork sausage, cut into ½-inch slices**
- **1 large green pepper, cut into 2-inch-long strips (about 2 cups)**
- **1 large onion, sliced (about 1 cup)**
- **3 cloves garlic, minced**
- **1 can (10¾ ounces) Campbell's® Condensed Cheddar Cheese Soup**
- **½ cup milk**
- **2 cups penne pasta, cooked and drained**

1. Heat the oil in a 10-inch skillet over medium-high heat. Add the sausage and cook until well browned, stirring occasionally. Remove the sausage from the skillet. Pour off any fat.

2. Add the green pepper and onion to the skillet and cook until the vegetables are tender, stirring occasionally. Add the garlic and cook and stir for 1 minute. Stir in the soup and milk and heat to a boil. Return the sausage to the skillet. Reduce the heat to low. Cook until the sausage is cooked through, stirring occasionally.

3. Place the pasta into a large bowl. Add the sausage mixture and toss to coat.

Kitchen Tip

You may substitute hot Italian sausage for the sweet Italian sausage in this recipe.

Lasagna Roll-Ups

Makes 4 servings

PREP TIME
30 minutes

BAKE TIME
35 minutes

STAND TIME
10 minutes

- **1 cup ricotta cheese**
- **1 can (about 4 ounces) mushroom stems and pieces, drained**
- **½ cup refrigerated pesto sauce**
- **8 lasagna noodles, cooked and drained**
- **2 cups Prego® Traditional Italian Sauce *or* Tomato, Basil & Garlic Italian Sauce**
- **¾ cup Pace® Picante Sauce**
- **4 ounces shredded mozzarella cheese (about 1 cup)**

1. Stir the ricotta, mushrooms and pesto in a medium bowl. Top **each** noodle with **¼ cup** of the cheese mixture. Spread to the edges. Roll up like a jelly roll. Place the rolls seam-side down in a 2-quart shallow baking dish.

2. Stir the Italian sauce and picante sauce in a small bowl and pour the mixture over the roll-ups.

3. Bake at 400°F. for 30 minutes or until they're hot and bubbling. Top with the mozzarella cheese. Bake for 5 minutes or until the cheese is melted. Let stand for 10 minutes.

3-Cheese Pasta Bake

Makes 4 servings

PREP TIME
20 minutes

BAKE TIME
20 minutes

Kitchen Tip

Substitute 2 cups of your favorite shredded cheese for the two-cheese blend.

- **1 can (10¾ ounces) Campbell's® Condensed Cream of Mushroom Soup (Regular *or* 98% Fat Free)**
- **1 package (8 ounces) shredded two-cheese blend (about 2 cups)**
- **⅓ cup grated Parmesan cheese**
- **1 cup milk**
- **¼ teaspoon ground black pepper**
- **3 cups corkscrew-shaped pasta (rotini), cooked and drained**

1. Stir the soup, cheeses, milk and black pepper in a 1½-quart casserole. Stir in the pasta.

2. Bake at 400°F. for 20 minutes or until the mixture is hot and bubbling.

Tortellini-Vegetable Toss

Makes 4 servings

1 jar (24 ounces) Prego® Chunky Garden Combination Italian Sauce

1 bag (16 ounces) frozen vegetable combination (broccoli, cauliflower, carrots)

1 package (16 ounces) frozen cheese-filled tortellini, cooked and drained

Grated Parmesan cheese

1. Heat the Italian sauce in a 3-quart saucepan over medium heat to a boil. Stir in the vegetables. Cover and cook for 10 minutes or until the vegetables are tender-crisp, stirring occasionally.

2. Put the tortellini in a large serving bowl. Pour the vegetable mixture over the tortellini. Toss to coat. Serve with the cheese.

PREP TIME
5 minutes

COOK TIME
15 minutes

Hearty Chicken & Noodle Casserole

Makes 4 servings

PREP TIME
15 minutes

BAKE TIME
25 minutes

- 1 can (10¾ ounces) Campbell's® Condensed Cream of Mushroom Soup (Regular *or* 98% Fat Free)
- ½ cup milk
- 1 cup frozen mixed vegetables
- 2 cups cubed cooked chicken
- 2 cups medium egg noodles, cooked and drained
- ¼ cup grated Parmesan cheese
- ¼ teaspoon ground black pepper
- ½ cup shredded Cheddar cheese

1. Heat the oven to 400°F. Stir the soup, milk, vegetables, chicken, noodles, Parmesan cheese and black pepper in a 1½-quart casserole.

2. Bake for 25 minutes or until the chicken mixture is hot and bubbling. Stir the chicken mixture. Top with the cheese. Let stand until the cheese is melted.

Kitchen Tip

Easy casseroles like this one are a simple way to transform leftovers. Cooked chicken, turkey or ham will all work in this recipe.

Baked Ziti Supreme

Makes 6 servings

- **1 pound ground beef**
- **1 medium onion, chopped (about ½ cup)**
- **1 jar (24 ounces) Prego® Fresh Mushroom Italian Sauce**
- **1½ cups shredded mozzarella cheese (6 ounces)**
- **5 cups medium tube-shaped pasta (ziti), cooked and drained**
- **¼ cup grated Parmesan cheese**

1. Cook the beef and onion in a 4-quart saucepan over medium-high heat until the beef is well browned, stirring often to separate the meat. Pour off any fat.

2. Stir the Italian sauce, **1 cup** mozzarella cheese and pasta in the saucepan. Spoon the mixture into a 3-quart shallow baking dish. Sprinkle with the remaining mozzarella cheese and Parmesan cheese. Bake at 350°F. for 30 minutes or until hot and bubbling.

PREP TIME
25 minutes

BAKE TIME
30 minutes

Extra-Easy Spinach Lasagna

Makes 8 servings

PREP TIME
20 minutes

BAKE TIME
50 minutes

STAND TIME
10 minutes

Kitchen Tip

To thaw the spinach, microwave on HIGH for 3 minutes, breaking apart with a fork halfway through heating.

- **1 container (15 ounces) ricotta cheese**
- **1 package (10 ounces) frozen chopped spinach, thawed and well drained**
- **8 ounces shredded mozzarella cheese (about 2 cups)**
- **1 jar (24 ounces) Prego® Fresh Mushroom Italian Sauce**
- **6 *uncooked* lasagna noodles**
- **¼ cup water**

1. Stir the ricotta, spinach and **1 cup** mozzarella cheese in a medium bowl.

2. Spread **1 cup** Italian sauce in a 2-quart shallow baking dish. Top with **3** lasagna noodles and **half** the spinach mixture. Repeat the layers. Top with the remaining sauce. Slowly pour water around the inside edges of the baking dish. **Cover**.

3. Bake at 400°F. for 40 minutes. Uncover the dish. Sprinkle with the remaining mozzarella cheese. Bake for 10 minutes or until the lasagna is hot and bubbling. Let stand for 10 minutes.

Creamy Pesto Chicken & Bow Ties

Makes 4 servings

2 tablespoons butter

4 skinless, boneless chicken breast halves, cut into cubes

1 can (10¾ ounces) Campbell's® Condensed Cream of Chicken Soup (Regular *or* 98% Fat Free)

½ cup milk

½ cup prepared pesto sauce

3 cups bow tie pasta (farfalle), cooked and drained

1. Heat the butter in a 10-inch skillet over medium-high heat. Add the chicken and cook until well browned, stirring often.

2. Stir the soup, milk and pesto in the skillet and heat to a boil. Reduce the heat to low. Cook for 5 minutes or until the chicken is cooked through. Stir in the pasta and cook until the mixture is hot and bubbling.

PREP TIME
10 minutes

COOK TIME
20 minutes

Family Spaghetti Pie

Makes 6 servings

PREP TIME
25 minutes

BAKE TIME
30 minutes

STAND TIME
5 minutes

- **1 pound ground beef**
- **1 cup Pace® Picante Sauce**
- **1 cup Prego® Fresh Mushroom Italian Sauce**
- **⅓ of a 16-ounce package spaghetti, cooked and drained (about 3 cups)**
- **⅓ cup grated Parmesan cheese**
- **1 egg, beaten**
- **1 tablespoon butter, melted**
- **1 cup ricotta cheese**
- **4 ounces shredded mozzarella cheese (about 1 cup)**

1. Cook the beef in a 10-inch skillet over medium-high heat until meat is well browned, stirring frequently to separate the meat. Pour off any fat. Stir the picante sauce and Italian sauce into the skillet and cook until hot and bubbling.

2. Stir the spaghetti, Parmesan cheese, egg and butter in a medium bowl. Spread the mixture on the bottom and up the side of a greased 10-inch pie plate. Spread the ricotta in the spaghetti shell. Top with the beef mixture.

3. Bake at 350°F. for 30 minutes or until the mixture is hot and bubbling. Sprinkle with the mozzarella cheese. Let stand for 5 minutes before serving. Cut into **6** wedges.

Ranchero Macaroni Bake

Makes 8 servings

- 1 can (26 ounces) Campbell's® Condensed Cream of Mushroom Soup (Regular ***or*** 98% Fat Free)
- 1 cup milk
- 1 cup Pace® Picante Sauce
- 3 cups shredded Cheddar cheese ***or*** Monterey Jack cheese
- 3 cups elbow pasta, cooked and drained
- 1 cup coarsely crushed tortilla chips

PREP TIME
20 minutes

BAKE TIME
25 minutes

1. Stir the soup, milk, picante sauce, cheese and pasta in a 3-quart shallow baking dish.

2. Bake at 400°F. for 20 minutes or until the pasta mixture is hot and bubbling. Stir the pasta mixture. Sprinkle with the tortilla chips.

3. Bake for 5 minutes or until the tortillas chips are golden brown.

Kitchen Tip

Makes 12 side-dish servings.

Easy Pasta Primavera

Makes 4 servings

PREP TIME
20 minutes

COOK TIME
15 minutes

- **2 tablespoons cornstarch**
- **1¾ cups Swanson® Natural Goodness® Chicken Broth**
- **1 teaspoon dried oregano leaves, crushed**
- **¼ teaspoon garlic powder *or* 2 garlic cloves, minced**
- **2 cups broccoli florets**
- **2 medium carrots, sliced (about 1 cup)**
- **1 medium onion, cut into wedges**
- **1 medium tomato, diced (about 1 cup)**
- **½ of a 1-pound package thin spaghetti, cooked and drained (about 4 cups)**
- **3 tablespoons grated Parmesan cheese**

1. Stir the cornstarch and **¾ cup** broth in a small bowl until the mixture is smooth.

2. Heat the remaining broth, oregano, garlic powder, broccoli, carrots and onion in a 4-quart saucepan over medium heat to a boil. Reduce the heat to low. Cover and cook for 5 minutes or until the vegetables are tender-crisp.

3. Stir the cornstarch mixture in the saucepan. Cook and stir until the mixture boils and thickens. Stir in the tomato. Add the spaghetti and toss to coat. Sprinkle with the cheese.

Miracle Lasagna

Makes 6 servings

1 jar (24 ounces) Prego® Traditional Italian Sauce *or* Tomato, Basil & Garlic Italian Sauce
6 ***uncooked*** lasagna noodles
1 container (15 ounces) ricotta cheese
8 ounces shredded mozzarella cheese (about 2 cups)
¼ cup grated Parmesan cheese

PREP TIME
10 minutes

BAKE TIME
1 hour

STAND TIME
5 minutes

1. Spread **about 1 cup** of the Italian sauce in a 2-quart shallow baking dish. Top with **3 uncooked** noodles, ricotta, **1 cup** mozzarella cheese, Parmesan cheese and **1 cup** sauce. Top with the remaining **3 uncooked** noodles and the remaining sauce. Cover the dish.

2. Bake at 375°F. for 1 hour. Uncover the dish and top with the remaining mozzarella cheese. Let stand for 5 minutes.

Baked Macaroni and Cheese

Makes 4 servings

PREP TIME
20 minutes

BAKE TIME
20 minutes

- **1 can (10¾ ounces) Campbell's® Condensed Cheddar Cheese Soup**
- **½ soup can milk**
- **⅛ teaspoon ground black pepper**
- **2 cups corkscrew-shaped pasta (rotini) *or* shell-shaped pasta**
- **1 tablespoon dry bread crumbs**
- **2 teaspoons butter, melted**

1. Stir the soup, milk, black pepper and pasta in a 1-quart baking dish.

2. Stir the bread crumbs and butter in a small bowl. Sprinkle the bread crumb mixture over the pasta mixture.

3. Bake at 400°F. for 20 minutes or until the pasta mixture is hot and bubbling.

Broccoli & Noodles Supreme

Makes 5 servings

- 3 cups ***uncooked*** medium egg noodles
- 2 cups fresh ***or*** frozen broccoli florets
- 1 can (10¾ ounces) Campbell's® Condensed Cream of Chicken Soup (Regular ***or*** 98% Fat Free)
- ½ cup sour cream
- ⅓ cup grated Parmesan cheese
- ⅛ teaspoon ground black pepper

PREP TIME
10 minutes

COOK TIME
25 minutes

1. Cook the noodles according to the package directions. Add the broccoli for the last 5 minutes of cooking time. Drain the noodle mixture well in a colander. Return the noodle mixture to the saucepan.

2. Stir the soup, sour cream, cheese and black pepper in the saucepan and cook over medium heat until the mixture is hot and bubbling, stirring often.

Super Suppers

Skillet Vegetable Lasagna

Makes 4 servings

PREP TIME
10 minutes

COOK TIME
15 minutes

Kitchen Tip

You can try using 4 ounces mozzarella cut into very thin slices instead of the shredded mozzarella.

- **2¾ cups Swanson® Vegetable Broth (Regular *or* Certified Organic)**
- **15 *uncooked* oven-ready (no-boil) lasagna noodles**
- **1 can (10¾ ounces) Campbell's® Condensed Cream of Mushroom Soup (Regular *or* 98% Fat Free)**
- **1 can (about 14.5 ounces) diced tomatoes, undrained**
- **1 package (10 ounces) frozen chopped spinach, thawed and well drained**
- **1 cup ricotta cheese**
- **1 cup shredded mozzarella cheese (about 4 ounces)**

1. Heat the broth in a 12-inch skillet over medium-high heat to a boil. Break the noodles into pieces and add to the broth. Reduce the heat to low. Cook for 3 minutes or until the noodles are tender.

2. Stir the soup, tomatoes and spinach in the skillet. Cook for 5 minutes or until the mixture is hot and bubbling.

3. Remove the skillet from the heat. Spoon the ricotta cheese on top and sprinkle with the mozzarella cheese.

Skillet Chicken & Rice

Makes 4 servings

PREP TIME
5 minutes

COOK TIME
35 minutes

1 pound skinless, boneless chicken breasts, cut into cubes

1¾ cups Swanson® Chicken Stock

½ teaspoon dried basil leaves, crushed

½ teaspoon garlic powder

¾ cup *uncooked* regular long-grain white rice

1 package (16 ounces) frozen vegetable combination (broccoli, cauliflower, carrots)

1. Cook the chicken in a 10-inch nonstick skillet over medium-high heat until well browned, stirring often. Remove the chicken from the skillet.

2. Stir in the stock, basil and garlic powder and heat to a boil. Stir in the rice. Reduce the heat to low. Cover and cook for 5 minutes.

3. Stir in the vegetables. Return the chicken to the skillet. Cover and cook for 15 minutes or until the chicken is cooked through and the rice is tender.

Zesty Turkey & Rice

Makes 4 servings

- **2 cups Swanson® Chicken Stock**
- **1 teaspoon dried basil leaves, crushed**
- **¼ teaspoon garlic powder**
- **¼ teaspoon hot pepper sauce**
- **1 can (about 14.5 ounces) stewed tomatoes**
- **¾ cup *uncooked* regular long-grain white rice**
- **1 cup frozen peas**
- **2 cups cubed, cooked turkey *or* chicken**

1. Heat the stock, basil, garlic powder, hot pepper sauce and tomatoes in a 2½-quart saucepan over medium heat to a boil. Stir in the rice. Reduce the heat to low. Cover and cook for 20 minutes.

2. Stir in the peas and turkey. Cover and cook for 5 minutes or until the rice is done.

PREP TIME
5 minutes

COOK TIME
30 minutes

Chicken Cacciatore & Pasta

Makes 4 servings

PREP TIME
10 minutes

COOK TIME
30 minutes

- **1 tablespoon vegetable oil**
- **4 skinless, boneless chicken breast halves (about 1 pound)**
- **1¾ cups Swanson® Chicken Stock**
- **1 teaspoon dried oregano leaves, crushed**
- **1 teaspoon garlic powder**
- **1 can (14.5 ounces) diced tomatoes**
- **1 small green pepper, cut into 2-inch-long strips (about 1 cup)**
- **1 medium onion, cut into wedges**
- **¼ teaspoon ground black pepper**
- **2½ cups *uncooked* medium shell-shaped pasta**

1. Heat the oil in a 10-inch skillet over medium-high heat. Add the chicken and cook for 10 minutes or until well browned on both sides.

2. Stir the stock, oregano, garlic powder, tomatoes, green pepper, onion and black pepper in the skillet and heat to a boil. Stir in the pasta. Reduce the heat to low. Cover and cook for 15 minutes or until the pasta is tender.

Chicken Mushroom Risotto

Makes 4 servings

- **3 skinless, boneless chicken breast halves (about ¾ pound), cut into cubes**
- **1 small onion, finely chopped (about ¼ cup)**
- **1 small carrot, chopped (about ¼ cup)**
- **1 cup *uncooked* regular long-grain white rice**
- **1 can (10¾ ounces) Campbell's® Healthy Request® Condensed Cream of Mushroom Soup**
- **1¾ cups Swanson® Chicken Stock**
- **⅛ teaspoon ground black pepper**
- **½ cup frozen peas**

1. Cook the chicken in a 10-inch nonstick skillet over medium-high heat until well browned, stirring often. Remove the chicken from the skillet.

2. Stir the onion, carrot and rice in the skillet and cook and stir until the rice is browned.

3. Stir in the soup, stock and black pepper and heat to a boil. Reduce the heat to low. Cover and cook for 15 minutes.

4. Stir in the peas. Return the chicken to the skillet. Cover and cook for 5 minutes or until the chicken is cooked through and the rice is tender.

PREP TIME
15 minutes

COOK TIME
35 minutes

Asian-Style Rice

Makes 4 servings

PREP TIME
10 minutes

COOK TIME
30 minutes

Vegetable cooking spray
- **1 egg, beaten**
- **¾ cup *uncooked* regular long-grain white rice**
- **1¾ cups Swanson® Chicken Broth (Regular, Natural Goodness® *or* Certified Organic)**
- **1 tablespoon soy sauce**
- **½ teaspoon garlic powder**
- **¼ teaspoon ground ginger**
- **1 medium carrot, sliced (about ½ cup)**
- **2 green onions, thickly sliced (about ¼ cup)**
- **½ cup frozen peas**

1. Spray a 10-inch nonstick skillet with vegetable cooking spray and heat for 1 minute over medium heat. Add the egg and cook until set. Remove the egg from the skillet.

2. Remove the skillet from the heat and spray with cooking spray. Add the rice and cook until browned, stirring often.

3. Stir the broth, soy sauce, garlic, ginger and carrot in the skillet and heat to a boil. Reduce the heat to low. Cover and cook for 15 minutes. Stir the onions and peas in the skillet. Cook for 5 minutes or until they're tender. Stir in the egg and heat through.

Maple Dijon Chicken

Makes 4 servings

PREP TIME
10 minutes

COOK TIME
25 minutes

- **1 tablespoon olive oil**
- **4 skinless, boneless chicken breast halves (about 1 pound)**
- **2 shallots, chopped (about ½ cup)**
- **2 cloves garlic, minced**
- **1 cup Swanson® Chicken Stock**
- **⅓ cup maple-flavored syrup**
- **1 tablespoon Dijon-style mustard**
- **⅛ teaspoon crushed red pepper**

1. Heat the oil in a 12-inch skillet over medium-high heat. Add the chicken and cook for 15 minutes or until well browned on both sides and cooked through. Remove the chicken from the skillet.

2. Add the shallots and garlic to the skillet and cook until they're tender. Stir in the stock, syrup, mustard and pepper and heat to a boil. Reduce the heat to low. Cook for 10 minutes or until the stock mixture is slightly thickened and reduced to **about 1 cup**. Serve the stock mixture over the chicken.

Golden Chicken & Autumn Vegetables

Makes 4 servings

PREP TIME
10 minutes

COOK TIME
30 minutes

- **1 tablespoon vegetable oil**
- **4 skinless, boneless chicken breast halves (about 1 pound)**
- **1 cup Swanson® Chicken Stock**
- **2 tablespoons minced garlic**
- **½ teaspoon dried rosemary leaves, crushed**
- **½ teaspoon dried thyme leaves, crushed**
- **¼ teaspoon ground black pepper**
- **2 large sweet potatoes, cut into ½-inch pieces**
- **2 cups fresh *or* frozen whole green beans**

1. Heat the oil in a 12-inch skillet over medium-high heat. Add the chicken and cook for 10 minutes or until well browned on both sides. Remove the chicken from the skillet.

2. Stir the stock, garlic, rosemary, thyme, black pepper, potatoes and green beans in the skillet and heat to a boil. Cook for 5 minutes.

3. Reduce the heat to low. Return the chicken to the skillet. Cover and cook for 10 minutes or until the chicken is cooked through and the potatoes are tender. Season as desired.

Herbed Chicken Dijon with Wine: Add **¼ cup** white wine, **1 teaspoon** lemon juice and **2 tablespoons** Dijon-style mustard with the stock in Step 2. Substitute Yukon Gold potatoes for the sweet potatoes.

Kitchen Tip

You can substitute 4 bone-in chicken breast halves (about 2 pounds), skin removed, for the skinless, boneless chicken. Increase the cooking time to 20 minutes or until the chicken is cooked through.

Savory Sausage & Rice Skillet

Makes 6 servings

PREP TIME
15 minutes

COOK TIME
1 hour

- **1 pound sweet Italian pork sausage, cut into 1-inch pieces**
- **2 stalks celery, sliced (about 1 cup)**
- **1 large onion, chopped (about 1 cup)**
- **1 medium green pepper, cut into 2-inch-long strips (about 1½ cups)**
- **1 medium red pepper, cut into 2-inch-long strips (about 1½ cups)**
- **3 cloves garlic, minced**
- **1 teaspoon dried thyme leaves, crushed *or* 1 tablespoon chopped fresh thyme leaves**
- **1 cup *uncooked* regular brown rice**
- **½ cup *uncooked* wild rice**
- **3½ cups Swanson® Chicken Stock**
- **2 tablespoons chopped fresh parsley**

1. Cook the sausage in a 12-inch nonstick skillet over medium-high heat until well browned, stirring often. Stir in the celery, onion, peppers, garlic and thyme and cook until the vegetables are tender.

2. Stir in the brown rice, wild rice and stock and heat to a boil. Reduce the heat to low. Cover and cook for 45 minutes or until the sausage is cooked through and the rice is tender. Stir in the parsley.

Brothy Shrimp & Rice Scampi

Makes 4 servings

3½ cups Swanson® Chicken Stock

¾ cup *uncooked* regular long-grain white rice

1 tablespoon olive oil

1 pound fresh *or* frozen large shrimp, peeled and deveined

4 cloves garlic, minced

2 tablespoons lemon juice

2 medium green onions, thinly sliced (about ¼ cup)

1. Heat the stock in a 2-quart saucepan over medium-high heat to a boil. Stir in the rice. Reduce the heat to low. Cover and cook for 20 minutes or until the rice is tender.

2. Heat the oil in a 10-inch skillet over medium-high heat. Add the shrimp and garlic. Cook and stir for 5 minutes or until the shrimp are cooked through.

3. Divide the shrimp among **4** serving bowls. Stir the lemon juice into the saucepan. Pour the rice mixture over the shrimp. Top with the green onions.

PREP TIME
15 minutes

COOK TIME
25 minutes

Citrus Chicken and Rice

Makes 4 servings

PREP TIME
5 minutes

COOK TIME
35 minutes

4 **skinless, boneless chicken breast halves (about 1 pound)**
1¾ **cups Swanson® Chicken Stock**
¾ **cup orange juice**
1 **medium onion, chopped (about ½ cup)**
1 **cup *uncooked* regular long-grain white rice**
3 **tablespoons chopped fresh parsley**

1. Cook the chicken in a 10-inch nonstick skillet over medium-high heat for 10 minutes or until well browned on both sides. Remove the chicken from the skillet.

2. Stir the stock, orange juice, onion and rice in the skillet and heat to a boil. Reduce the heat to low. Cover and cook for 10 minutes.

3. Return the chicken to the skillet. Cover and cook for 10 minutes or until the chicken is cooked through and the rice is tender. Stir in the parsley.

Kitchen Tip

For a special touch, cook orange slices in a nonstick skillet over medium-high heat until they're lightly browned. Serve over the chicken.

Pork Chop Skillet Dinner

Makes 4 servings

PREP TIME
10 minutes

COOK TIME
40 minutes

- **1 tablespoon olive oil**
- **4 bone-in pork chops, ¾-inch thick *each***
- **1 medium onion, chopped (about ½ cup)**
- **1 cup *uncooked* regular long-grain white rice**
- **1¼ cups Swanson® Chicken Stock**
- **1 cup orange juice**
- **3 tablespoons chopped fresh parsley**
- **¼ teaspoon ground black pepper**
- **4 orange slices**

1. Heat the oil in a 12-inch skillet over medium-high heat. Add the pork and cook until well browned on both sides.

2. Add the onion and rice to the skillet. Cook until the rice is lightly browned.

3. Stir in the stock, orange juice, **2 tablespoons** parsley and black pepper and heat to a boil. Reduce the heat to low. Cover and cook for 20 minutes or until the pork is cooked through and the rice is tender. Top with the orange slices and sprinkle with the remaining parsley.

Quick Chicken Stir-Fry

Makes 4 servings

PREP TIME
15 minutes

COOK TIME
15 minutes

- **2 tablespoons cornstarch**
- **1¾ cups Swanson® Chicken Stock**
- **1 tablespoon soy sauce**
- **½ teaspoon ground ginger**
- **4 cups cut-up vegetables***
- **2 cans (4.5 ounces *each*) Swanson® Premium White Chunk Chicken Breast in Water, drained**
- **4 cups hot cooked rice**

****Use a combination of broccoli florets, green onions cut into 1-inch pieces, sliced carrots* and *sliced celery* or *broccoli florets, sliced carrots* and *green* or *red pepper strips.***

1. Stir the cornstarch, **1 cup** stock, soy sauce and ginger in a small bowl until the mixture is smooth.

2. Heat the vegetables and remaining stock in a 10-inch nonstick skillet over medium-high heat to a boil. Reduce the heat to low. Cover and cook for 5 minutes or until the vegetables are tender-crisp.

3. Stir the cornstarch mixture in the skillet. Cook and stir until the mixture boils and thickens. Stir in the chicken and cook until the mixture is hot and bubbling. Serve the chicken mixture over the rice.

Poached Halibut with Pineapple Salsa

Makes 4 servings

- 1 can (about 15 ounces) pineapple chunks in juice, undrained
- 1 seedless cucumber, peeled and diced (about 1⅔ cups)
- 1 medium red pepper, chopped (about ¾ cup)
- 2 tablespoons chopped red onion
- 1 teaspoon white wine vinegar
- 1 teaspoon hot pepper sauce (optional)
- 1¾ cups Swanson® Chicken Stock
- ¼ cup white wine
- 4 halibut fillets (about 1½ pounds)

1. Drain the pineapple and reserve ⅔ **cup** juice.

2. Stir the pineapple chunks, cucumber, red pepper, red onion, vinegar and hot pepper sauce, if desired, in a medium bowl.

3. Heat the stock, wine and reserved pineapple juice in a 12-inch skillet over medium-high heat to a boil. Add the fish to the skillet. Reduce the heat to low. Cover and cook for 10 minutes or until the fish flakes easily when tested with a fork. Serve the fish with the pineapple salsa.

PREP TIME
10 minutes

COOK TIME
15 minutes

Pan-Seared Salmon in Peach Mango Sauce

Makes 4 servings

PREP TIME
20 minutes

COOK TIME
30 minutes

- **4 salmon fillets, ¾-inch thick (about 1 pound)**
- **Vegetable cooking spray**
- **1 large red pepper, chopped (about 1 cup)**
- **1 clove garlic, minced**
- **1½ cups V8 V-Fusion® Peach Mango Juice**
- **1 mango, peeled, seeded and chopped (about 1¼ cups)**
- **¼ cup honey**
- **2 tablespoons cornstarch**
- **1 tablespoon lime juice**
- **¼ teaspoon cracked black pepper**
- **4 cups fresh baby spinach**
- **2 tablespoons chopped fresh cilantro leaves**
- **2 cups cooked regular brown rice**

1. Season the salmon as desired.

2. Spray a 12-inch skillet with the cooking spray and heat over medium-high heat for 1 minute. Add the salmon, skin-side up, and cook for about 5 minutes or until well browned. Turn the salmon over and cook for 4 minutes or until it flakes easily when tested with a fork. Remove the salmon from the skillet and keep warm.

3. Add the red pepper and garlic to the skillet and cook over medium heat until the pepper is tender-crisp.

4. Stir the juice, mango, honey, cornstarch, lime juice and black pepper in a small bowl. Stir the juice mixture and the spinach into the skillet. Cook for 2 minutes or until the mixture boils and thickens. Stir in the cilantro. Serve over the salmon. Serve with the rice.

Chicken Balsamico

Makes 4 servings

PREP TIME
10 minutes

COOK TIME
20 minutes

- **1 tablespoon olive oil**
- **4 skinless, boneless chicken breast halves (about 1 pound)**
- **1 clove garlic, minced**
- **3 tablespoons balsamic vinegar**
- **¾ cup water**
- **1 can (10¾ ounces) Campbell's® Condensed Cream of Chicken Soup (Regular *or* 98% Fat Free)**
- **1 cup diced plum tomatoes *or* ½ cup thinly sliced sun-dried tomatoes**
- **½ cup sliced pitted kalamata olives**
- **½ teaspoon dried oregano leaves, crushed**
- **¼ cup crumbled feta cheese**
- **Hot cooked orzo pasta**

1. Heat the oil in a 10-inch skillet over medium-high heat. Add the chicken and cook for 10 minutes or until well browned on both sides. Remove the chicken from the skillet.

2. Stir the garlic, vinegar and water in the skillet. Cook and stir for 1 minute. Stir in the soup, tomatoes, olives, if desired, and oregano and heat to a boil. Return the chicken to the skillet. Reduce the heat to low. Cook for 5 minutes or until the chicken is cooked through. Sprinkle with the cheese. Serve the chicken and sauce with the orzo.

Quick & Easy Fare

Quick Skillet Chicken & Macaroni Parmesan

Makes 6 servings

PREP TIME
15 minutes

COOK TIME
15 minutes

STAND TIME
5 minutes

- **1 jar (24 ounces) Prego® Traditional Italian Sauce *or* Tomato, Basil & Garlic Italian Sauce**
- **¼ cup grated Parmesan cheese**
- **1 can (12.5 ounces) Swanson® Premium White Chunk Chicken Breast in Water, drained**
- **2 cups elbow pasta, cooked and drained (about 3 cups)**
- **1 cup shredded mozzarella cheese (about 4 ounces)**

1. Heat the Italian sauce, Parmesan cheese, chicken and pasta in a 10-inch skillet over medium-high heat to a boil. Reduce the heat to medium and cook for 10 minutes or until the mixture is hot and bubbling, stirring occasionally.

2. Sprinkle with the mozzarella cheese. Let stand for 5 minutes or until the cheese is melted.

Easy Beef & Pasta

Makes 4 servings

PREP TIME
5 minutes

COOK TIME
20 minutes

- **1 tablespoon vegetable oil**
- **1 pound boneless beef sirloin steak, ¾-inch thick, cut into very thin strips**
- **1 can (10¾ ounces) Campbell's® Condensed Tomato Soup (Regular *or* Healthy Request®)**
- **½ cup water**
- **1 bag (about 16 ounces) frozen vegetable pasta blend**

1. Heat the oil in a 10-inch skillet over medium-high heat. Add the beef and cook until well browned, stirring often. Pour off any fat.

2. Stir the soup, water and vegetable pasta blend in the skillet and heat to a boil. Reduce the heat to low. Cover and cook for 5 minutes or until the beef is cooked through.

Quick Chicken Mozzarella Sandwiches

Makes 4 servings

1½ cups Prego® Three Cheese Italian Sauce
4 refrigerated *or* thawed frozen cooked breaded chicken cutlets
4 slices mozzarella cheese
4 round hard rolls

1. Heat the Italian sauce in a 10-inch skillet over medium heat to a boil. Place the chicken in the sauce. Reduce the heat to low. Cover and cook for 5 minutes or until the chicken is heated through.

2. Top the chicken with the cheese. Cover and cook until the cheese is melted. Serve on the rolls.

PREP TIME
5 minutes

COOK TIME
15 minutes

Skillet Chicken Parmesan

Makes 6 servings

PREP TIME
5 minutes

COOK TIME
20 minutes

STAND TIME
5 minutes

- ¼ cup grated Parmesan cheese
- 1½ cups Prego® Traditional ***or*** Organic Tomato & Basil Italian Sauce
- 1 tablespoon olive oil
- 1½ pounds skinless, boneless chicken breast halves
- 1½ cups shredded part-skim mozzarella cheese (about 6 ounces)

1. Stir **3 tablespoons** of the Parmesan cheese and Italian sauce in a small bowl.

2. Heat the oil in a 12-inch skillet over medium-high heat. Add the chicken and cook for 10 minutes or until well browned on both sides.

3. Pour the sauce mixture over the chicken, turning to coat with the sauce. Reduce the heat to low. Cover and cook for 10 minutes or until chicken is cooked through.

4. Top with the mozzarella cheese and the remaining Parmesan cheese. Let stand for 5 minutes or until the cheese is melted.

Beef Taco Skillet

Makes 4 servings

PREP TIME
5 minutes

COOK TIME
20 minutes

- **1 pound ground beef**
- **1 can (10¾ ounces) Campbell's® Condensed Tomato Soup (Regular *or* Healthy Request®)**
- **½ cup Pace® Picante Sauce**
- **½ cup water**
- **6 flour tortillas (6-inch), cut into 1-inch pieces**
- **½ cup shredded Cheddar cheese**

1. Cook the beef in a 10-inch skillet over medium-high heat until well browned, stirring often to separate the meat. Pour off any fat.

2. Stir the soup, picante sauce, water and tortillas in the skillet and heat to a boil. Reduce the heat to low. Cook for 5 minutes. Stir the beef mixture. Top with the cheese.

Creamy Mexican Fiesta: Stir in **½ cup** sour cream with the soup.

Ranchero Style: Use corn tortillas instead of flour tortillas and shredded Mexican cheese blend instead of Cheddar.

French Onion Burgers

Makes 4 servings

PREP TIME
5 minutes

COOK TIME
20 minutes

Kitchen Tip

You can also serve these burgers in a bowl atop a mound of hot mashed potatoes with some of the soup mixture poured over.

1 pound ground beef

1 can (10½ ounces) Campbell's® Condensed French Onion Soup

4 slices cheese

4 Pepperidge Farm® Classic Sandwich Buns, split

1. Shape the beef into **4** (½-inch-thick) burgers.

2. Heat a 10-inch skillet over medium-high heat. Add the burgers and cook until well browned on both sides. Remove the burgers from the skillet. Pour off any fat.

3. Stir the soup in the skillet and heat to a boil. Return the burgers to the skillet. Reduce the heat to low. Cover and cook for 5 minutes or until desired doneness. Top the burgers with the cheese and cook until the cheese is melted. Serve the burgers on the buns with the soup mixture for dipping.

Cheeseburger Pasta

Makes 5 servings

1	**pound ground beef**
1	**can (10¾ ounces) Campbell's® Condensed Cheddar Cheese Soup**
1	**can (10¾ ounces) Campbell's® Condensed Tomato Soup (Regular *or* Healthy Request®)**
1½	**cups water**
2	**cups *uncooked* medium shell-shaped pasta**

1. Cook the beef in a 10-inch skillet over medium-high heat until well browned, stirring often to separate the meat. Pour off any fat.

2. Stir the soups, water and pasta in the skillet and heat to a boil. Reduce the heat to medium. Cook for 10 minutes or until the pasta is tender, stirring often.

PREP TIME
5 minutes

COOK TIME
20 minutes

Beef Stroganoff

Makes 4 servings

PREP TIME
10 minutes

COOK TIME
25 minutes

1 tablespoon vegetable oil

1 boneless beef sirloin steak *or* beef top round steak, ¾-inch thick (about 1 pound), cut into thin strips

1 medium onion, chopped (about ½ cup)

1 can (10¾ ounces) Campbell's® Condensed Cream of Mushroom Soup (Regular, 98% Fat Free *or* Healthy Request®)

½ teaspoon paprika

⅓ cup sour cream *or* plain yogurt

4 cups whole wheat *or* regular egg noodles, cooked and drained

Chopped fresh parsley

1. Heat the oil in a 12-inch nonstick skillet over medium-high heat. Add the beef and cook until well browned, stirring often. Remove the beef from the skillet. Pour off any fat.

2. Reduce the heat to medium. Add the onion to the skillet and cook until tender.

3. Stir the soup and paprika in the skillet and heat to a boil. Stir in the sour cream. Return the beef to the skillet and cook until the beef is cooked through. Serve the beef mixture over the noodles. Sprinkle with the parsley.

Quick Glazed Pork & Rice Skillet

Makes 4 servings

PREP TIME
5 minutes

COOK TIME
25 minutes

- **4 boneless pork chops, ¾-inch thick *each* (about 1 pound)**
- **3 cups Swanson® Chicken Stock**
- **¾ cup apricot preserves *or* orange marmalade**
- **1 tablespoon Dijon-style mustard**
- **2 cups *uncooked* instant white rice**

1. Cook the pork in a 12-inch nonstick skillet over medium-high heat until well browned on both sides. Remove the pork from the skillet.

2. Stir the stock, preserves and mustard in the skillet and heat to a boil. Reduce the heat to low. Stir in the rice. Return the pork to the skillet. Cover and cook for 10 minutes or until the pork is cooked through and the rice is tender.

Quick Chicken & Vegetable Stir-Fry

Makes 4 servings

PREP TIME
15 minutes

COOK TIME
15 minutes

- **2 tablespoons cornstarch**
- **1¾ cups Swanson® Chicken Stock**
- **1 tablespoon soy sauce**
- **1 tablespoon vegetable oil**
- **4 cups cut-up vegetables***
- **2 cloves garlic, minced**
- **1 can (12.5 ounces)** Swanson® Premium White Chunk Chicken Breast in Water, drained**
- **4 cups hot cooked rice**

Use a combination of broccoli florets, sliced carrots* **and *green* **or** *red pepper strips.*

***Or* **3** *cans (4.5 ounces* **each**).*

1. Stir the cornstarch, stock and soy sauce in a small bowl until the mixture is smooth.

2. Heat the oil in a 10-inch skillet over medium-high heat. Add the vegetables and cook until they're tender-crisp. Add the garlic and cook for 1 minute.

3. Stir the cornstarch mixture in the skillet. Reduce the heat to medium. Cook and stir until the mixture boils and thickens. Stir in the chicken and cook until the mixture is heated through. Serve the chicken mixture over the rice.

Crusted Tilapia Florentine

Makes 4 servings

- 1 egg
- 2 teaspoons water
- 1 cup Italian-seasoned dry bread crumbs
- 4 fresh tilapia fillets (about 4 ounces *each*)
- 2 tablespoons olive oil
- 2⅔ cups Prego® Traditional Italian Sauce
- 2 cups frozen chopped spinach
- Hot cooked noodles

1. Beat the egg and water with a fork in a shallow dish. Place the bread crumbs on a plate. Dip the fish in the egg mixture, then coat with the bread crumbs.

2. Heat the oil in a 12-inch skillet over medium-high heat. Add the fish and cook for 8 minutes, turning once or until the fish flakes easily when tested with a fork. Remove the fish and keep warm.

3. Stir the Italian sauce and spinach into the skillet. Heat to a boil. Reduce the heat to medium. Cook for 2 minutes or until the spinach is wilted. Serve the sauce over the fish. Serve with the noodles.

PREP TIME
10 minutes

COOK TIME
15 minutes

Dripping Roast Beef Sandwiches with Melted Provolone

Makes 4 servings

PREP TIME
5 minutes

COOK TIME
5 minutes

BAKE TIME
3 minutes

1 can (10½ ounces) Campbell's® Condensed French Onion Soup

1 tablespoon reduced-sodium Worcestershire sauce

¾ pound thinly sliced deli roast beef

4 Pepperidge Farm® Classic Soft Hoagie Rolls with Sesame Seeds

4 slices deli provolone cheese, cut in half

¼ cup drained hot *or* mild pickled banana pepper rings

1. Heat the oven to 400°F.

2. Heat the soup and Worcestershire in a 2-quart saucepan over medium-high heat to a boil. Add the beef and heat through, stirring occasionally.

3. Divide the beef evenly among the rolls. Top the beef with the cheese slices and place the sandwiches onto a baking sheet.

4. Bake for 3 minutes or until the sandwiches are toasted and the cheese is melted. Spoon the soup mixture onto the sandwiches. Top **each** sandwich with **1 tablespoon** pepper rings.

Kitchen Tip

You may substitute ½ of a 11.25-ounce package Pepperidge Farm® Texas Toast (4 slices), prepared according to package directions, for the rolls in this recipe. Serve the sandwiches open-faced.

Chicken Tetrazzini

Makes 4 servings

PREP TIME
20 minutes

COOK TIME
5 minutes

- **1 can (10¾ ounces) Campbell's® Condensed Cream of Mushroom Soup (Regular *or* 98% Fat Free)**
- **¾ cup water**
- **½ cup grated Parmesan cheese**
- **2 tablespoons chopped fresh parsley *or* 2 teaspoons dried parsley flakes**
- **¼ cup chopped red pepper *or* pimientos (optional)**
- **½ package (8 ounces) spaghetti, cooked and drained**
- **2 cans (4.5 ounces *each*) Swanson® Premium White Chunk Chicken Breast in Water, drained**

Heat the soup, water, cheese, parsley, red pepper, if desired, spaghetti and chicken in a 2-quart saucepan over medium heat until the mixture is hot and bubbling.

Broccoli & Garlic Penne Pasta

Makes 4 servings

PREP TIME
20 minutes

COOK TIME
10 minutes

- **1 cup Swanson® Chicken Broth (Regular, Natural Goodness® *or* Certified Organic)**
- **½ teaspoon dried basil leaves, crushed**
- **⅛ teaspoon ground black pepper**
- **2 cloves garlic, minced**
- **3 cups broccoli florets**
- **4½ cups penne pasta, cooked and drained**
- **1 tablespoon lemon juice**
- **2 tablespoons grated Parmesan cheese**

1. Heat the broth, basil, black pepper, garlic and broccoli in a 10-inch skillet over medium heat to a boil. Reduce the heat to low. Cover and cook until the broccoli is tender-crisp.

2. Add the pasta and lemon juice and toss to coat. Sprinkle the pasta mixture with the cheese.

Quick Chicken & Noodles

Makes 4 servings

PREP TIME
5 minutes

COOK TIME
25 minutes

- **4 skinless, boneless chicken breast halves (about 1 pound)**
- **½ teaspoon garlic powder**
- **⅛ teaspoon paprika**
- **1¾ cups Swanson® Chicken Stock**
- **½ teaspoon dried basil leaves, crushed**
- **¼ teaspoon ground black pepper**
- **2 cups frozen vegetable combination (broccoli, cauliflower, carrots)**
- **2 cups *uncooked* medium egg noodles**

1. Season the chicken with the garlic powder and paprika. Cook the chicken in a 12-inch nonstick skillet over medium-high heat until well browned on both sides.

2. Add the stock, basil, black pepper and vegetables to the skillet and heat to a boil. Stir in the noodles. Reduce the heat to low. Cover and cook for 10 minutes or until the chicken is cooked through and the noodles are tender.

Quick & Easy Chicken, Broccoli & Brown Rice

Makes 4 servings

PREP TIME
5 minutes

COOK TIME
20 minutes

- **1 tablespoon vegetable oil**
- **4 skinless, boneless chicken breast halves (about 1 pound)**
- **1 can (10¾ ounces) Campbell's® Condensed Cream of Chicken Soup (Regular, 98% Fat Free *or* Healthy Request®)**
- **1½ cups water**
- **¼ teaspoon paprika**
- **¼ teaspoon ground black pepper**
- **1½ cups *uncooked* instant brown rice***
- **2 cups fresh *or* frozen broccoli florets**

****Cooking times vary. To ensure best results, use instant whole grain brown rice.***

1. Heat the oil in a 10-inch skillet over medium-high heat. Add the chicken and cook for 10 minutes or until well browned on both sides. Remove the chicken from the skillet.

2. Stir the soup, water, paprika and black pepper in the skillet and heat to a boil.

3. Stir the rice and broccoli in the skillet. Reduce the heat to low. Return the chicken to the skillet. Sprinkle the chicken with additional paprika and black pepper. Cover and cook for 5 minutes or until the chicken is cooked through and the rice is tender.

2-Step Skillet Chicken Broccoli Divan

Makes 4 servings

1 tablespoon butter

4 skinless, boneless chicken breast halves (about 1 pound), cut into 1-inch pieces

3 cups fresh *or* frozen broccoli florets

1 can (10¾ ounces) Campbell's® Condensed Cream of Chicken Soup (Regular *or* 98% Fat Free)

½ cup milk

½ cup shredded Cheddar cheese

1. Heat the butter in a 10-inch skillet over medium-high heat. Add the chicken and cook until well browned, stirring often.

2. Stir the broccoli, soup and milk in the skillet. Reduce the heat to low. Cover and cook for 5 minutes or until the chicken is cooked through. Sprinkle with the cheese.

PREP TIME
10 minutes

COOK TIME
15 minutes

Kitchen Tip

Try this recipe with Campbell's® Cream of Mushroom Soup and shredded Swiss cheese.

Beef Teriyaki

Makes 4 servings

PREP TIME
10 minutes

COOK TIME
15 minutes

2 tablespoons cornstarch
1¾ cups Swanson® Beef Stock
2 tablespoons soy sauce
1 tablespoon packed brown sugar
½ teaspoon garlic powder
1 boneless beef sirloin steak
4 cups fresh *or* frozen broccoli florets
Hot cooked rice

1. Stir the cornstarch, stock, soy sauce, brown sugar and garlic powder in a small bowl until the mixture is smooth.

2. Stir-fry the beef in a 10-inch nonstick skillet over medium-high heat until well browned, stirring often. Pour off any fat.

3. Add the broccoli to the skillet and cook for 1 minute. Stir in the cornstarch mixture. Cook and stir until the mixture boils and thickens. Serve the beef mixture over the rice.

Kitchen Tip

To make slicing easier, freeze the beef for 1 hour before slicing.

contents

135

164

181

Chicken & Turkey

Picante Skillet Chicken

Makes 6 servings

PREP TIME
5 minutes

COOK TIME
20 minutes

1 tablespoon vegetable oil

6 skinless, boneless chicken breast halves (about 1½ pounds)

1 jar (16 ounces) Pace® Picante Sauce

6 cups hot cooked rice

1. Heat the oil in a 10-inch skillet over medium-high heat. Add the chicken and cook for 10 minutes or until well browned on both sides.

2. Stir the picante sauce in the skillet and heat to a boil. Reduce the heat to medium. Cover and cook for 5 minutes or until the chicken is cooked through. Serve the chicken and sauce with the rice.

Creamy Chicken Dijon

Makes 4 servings

PREP TIME
10 minutes

COOK TIME
20 minutes

- **1 tablespoon vegetable oil**
- **4 skinless, boneless chicken breast halves (about 1 pound)**
- **1 can (10¾ ounces) Campbell's® Condensed Cream of Chicken Soup (Regular *or* 98% Fat Free)**
- **½ cup water**
- **1 tablespoon coarse-grain Dijon-style mustard**
- **1 tablespoon dry white wine**
- **1 teaspoon dried parsley flakes**
- **1 teaspoon packed brown sugar**
- **½ teaspoon onion powder**
- **¼ teaspoon dried tarragon leaves, crushed**
- **Dash garlic powder**

1. Heat the oil in a 10-inch skillet over medium-high heat. Add the chicken and cook for 10 minutes or until well browned on both sides.

2. Stir the soup, water, mustard, wine, parsley, brown sugar, onion powder, tarragon and garlic powder in the skillet and heat to a boil. Reduce the heat to low. Cover and cook for 5 minutes or until the chicken is cooked through.

Quick Chicken Parmesan

Makes 4 servings

4 skinless, boneless chicken breast halves (about 1 pound)

2 cups Prego® Traditional Italian Sauce *or* Fresh Mushroom Italian Sauce

2 ounces shredded mozzarella cheese (about ½ cup)

2 tablespoons grated Parmesan cheese

½ of a 16-ounce package spaghetti, cooked and drained (about 4 cups)

1. Place the chicken in a 2-quart shallow baking dish. Top the chicken with the Italian sauce. Sprinkle with the mozzarella cheese and Parmesan cheese.

2. Bake at 400°F. for 25 minutes or until cooked through. Serve with the spaghetti.

PREP TIME
5 minutes

BAKE TIME
25 minutes

Creamy Mushroom-Garlic Chicken

Makes 4 servings

PREP TIME
5 minutes

COOK TIME
20 minutes

1 tablespoon vegetable oil

4 skinless, boneless chicken breast halves (about 1 pound)

1 can (10¾ ounces) Campbell's® Condensed Cream of Mushroom with Roasted Garlic Soup

½ cup milk

1. Heat the oil in a 10-inch skillet over medium-high heat. Add the chicken and cook for 10 minutes or until well browned on both sides.

2. Stir the soup and milk in the skillet and heat to a boil. Reduce the heat to low. Cover and cook for 5 minutes or until the chicken is cooked through.

For Creamy Herbed Chicken: Substitute Campbell's® Condensed Cream of Chicken with Herbs Soup for the Cream of Mushroom with Roasted Garlic.

Southwest Salsa Chicken with Fresh Greens

Makes 6 servings

PREP TIME
10 minutes

COOK TIME
20 minutes

- **1 tablespoon chili powder**
- **1 teaspoon ground cumin**
- **6 skinless, boneless chicken breasts (about 1½ pounds), cut into strips**
- **1 tablespoon olive oil**
- **1 cup Pace® Picante Sauce**
- **¼ cup water**
- **1 bag (about 7 ounces) mixed salad greens**

1. Stir the chili powder and cumin in a medium bowl. Add the chicken and toss to coat.

2. Heat the oil in a 12-inch skillet over medium-high heat. Add the chicken and cook for 15 minutes or until well browned and cooked through, stirring often. Remove the chicken from the skillet, cover and keep warm.

3. Stir the picante sauce and water in the skillet and cook until the mixture is hot and bubbling. Divide the greens among **6** plates. Top with the chicken and sauce mixture.

Turkey Broccoli Divan

Makes 4 servings

PREP TIME
10 minutes

BAKE TIME
20 minutes

4 cups cooked broccoli florets

1½ cups cubed cooked turkey

1 can (10¾ ounces) Campbell's® Condensed Cream of Chicken Soup (Regular *or* 98% Fat Free)

⅓ cup milk

½ cup shredded Cheddar cheese

2 tablespoons dry bread crumbs

1 tablespoon butter, melted

1. Place the broccoli and turkey into a 9-inch pie plate.

2. Stir the soup and milk in a small bowl. Pour the soup mixture over the turkey and broccoli. Top with the cheese.

3. Stir the bread crumbs and butter in a small bowl. Sprinkle over the cheese.

4. Bake at 450°F. for 20 minutes or until the mixture is hot and bubbling.

Crunchy Chicken and Gravy

Makes 4 servings

PREP TIME
10 minutes

BAKE TIME
20 minutes

COOK TIME
5 minutes

- **1 cup Pepperidge Farm® Herb Seasoned Stuffing, crushed**
- **2 tablespoons grated Parmesan cheese**
- **1 egg**
- **4 skinless, boneless chicken breast halves (about 1 pound)**
- **2 tablespoons butter, melted**
- **1 jar (12 ounces) Campbell's® Slow Roast Chicken Gravy**

1. Stir the stuffing and cheese on a plate. Beat the egg in a shallow dish with a fork or whisk. Dip the chicken into the egg. Coat the chicken with the stuffing mixture. Place the chicken onto a baking sheet. Drizzle with the butter.

2. Bake at 400°F. for 20 minutes or until the chicken is cooked through.

3. Heat the gravy in a 1-quart saucepan over medium heat until hot and bubbling. Serve the gravy with the chicken.

Turkey & Broccoli Alfredo

Makes 4 servings

PREP TIME
10 minutes

COOK TIME
20 minutes

½ package (8 ounces) linguine

1 cup fresh *or* frozen broccoli florets

1 can (10¾ ounces) Campbell's® Condensed Cream of Mushroom Soup (Regular *or* 98% Fat Free)

½ cup milk

½ cup grated Parmesan cheese

¼ teaspoon ground black pepper

2 cups cubed cooked turkey

1. Prepare the linguine according to the package directions in a 3-quart saucepan. Add the broccoli during the last 4 minutes of the cooking time. Drain the linguine mixture well in a colander. Return the linguine mixture to the saucepan.

2. Stir the soup, milk, cheese, black pepper and turkey in the saucepan and cook over medium heat until the mixture is hot and bubbling, stirring occasionally. Serve with additional Parmesan cheese.

Kitchen Tip

Substitute spaghetti for the linguine.

Barbecued Chicken Sandwiches

Makes 4 servings

- 1 tablespoon butter
- 1 small green pepper, chopped (about ½ cup) (optional)
- 1 small onion, chopped (about ¼ cup)
- ¼ cup chopped celery
- ½ cup barbecue sauce
- 2 cans (4.5 ounces ***each***) Swanson® Premium White Chunk Chicken Breast in Water, drained
- 4 Pepperidge Farm® Classic Sandwich Buns with Sesame Seeds, split and toasted

1. Heat the butter in a 2-quart saucepan over medium heat. Stir the green pepper, onion and celery in the saucepan and cook until tender.

2. Stir the barbecue sauce and chicken in the saucepan. Heat until the mixture is hot and bubbling. Divide the chicken mixture among the buns.

PREP TIME
10 minutes

COOK TIME
15 minutes

Cheesy Chicken Pizza

Makes 4 servings

PREP TIME
15 minutes

BAKE TIME
15 minutes

- 1 package (about 13 ounces) refrigerated pizza dough
- ½ cup Pace® Picante Sauce
- ½ cup Prego® Traditional Italian Sauce ***or*** Roasted Garlic & Herb Italian Sauce
- 1 cup chopped cooked chicken ***or*** turkey
- ½ cup sliced pitted ripe olives
- 2 green onions, sliced (about ¼ cup)
- 4 ounces shredded mozzarella cheese (about 1 cup)

1. Heat the oven to 425°F.

2. Unroll the dough onto a greased 12-inch pizza pan. Press the dough into a 12-inch circle. Pinch up the edge to form a rim.

3. Stir the picante sauce and Italian sauce in a small bowl. Spread the picante sauce mixture over the crust to the rim. Top with the chicken, olives, onions and cheese.

4. Bake for 15 minutes or until the cheese is melted and the crust is golden brown.

Kitchen Tip

For a crispier crust, prepare the dough as directed in step 2. Bake the dough for 5 minutes. Remove the dough from the oven and proceed as directed in steps 3 and 4.

Quick & Easy Chicken Quesadillas

Makes 8 servings

4 skinless, boneless chicken breast halves (about 1 pound), cut into cubes

1 can (10¾ ounces) Campbell's® Condensed Cream of Chicken Soup (Regular *or* 98% Fat Free)

½ cup Pace® Picante Sauce

½ cup shredded Monterey Jack cheese

1 teaspoon chili powder

8 flour tortillas (8-inch), warmed

1. Heat the oven to 425°F.

2. Cook the chicken in a 10-inch nonstick skillet over medium-high heat until well browned and cooked through, stirring often. Stir in the soup, picante sauce, cheese and chili powder and cook until the mixture is hot and bubbling.

3. Place the tortillas onto **2** baking sheets. Spread **about ⅓ cup** chicken mixture on **half** of **each** tortilla to within ½ inch of the edge. Brush the edges of the tortillas with water. Fold the tortillas over the filling and press the edges to seal.

4. Bake for 5 minutes or until the filling is hot. Cut the quesadillas into wedges.

PREP TIME
15 minutes

COOK TIME
15 minutes

BAKE TIME
5 minutes

Turkey Fajitas

Makes 6 servings

PREP TIME
20 minutes

COOK TIME
15 minutes

- 2 jars (12 ounces ***each***) Campbell's® Slow Roast Turkey Gravy
- 1 cup Pace® Picante Sauce
- 2 tablespoons vegetable oil
- 2 small green ***or*** red peppers, cut into 2-inch-long strips (about 2 cups)
- 2 medium onions, sliced (about 2 cups)
- 3 cups cooked turkey ***or*** chicken strips
- 12 flour tortillas (6-inch), warmed
- Sliced pitted ripe olives

1. Stir the gravy and picante sauce in a 3-quart saucepan.

2. Heat the oil in a 10-inch skillet over medium heat. Add the peppers and onions and cook until tender-crisp, stirring occasionally. Stir in **2 cups** gravy mixture and the turkey. Reduce the heat to low. Cook until the mixture is hot and bubbling.

3. Spoon ⅓ **cup** turkey mixture down the center of **each** tortilla. Fold the tortillas around the filling. Heat the remaining gravy mixture over medium heat until the mixture is hot and bubbling. Serve with the filled tortillas. Garnish with the olives.

Kitchen Tip

You can also use cooked steak strips and substitute beef gravy for the turkey gravy.

Chicken & Stir-Fry Vegetable Pizza

Makes 4 servings

PREP TIME
5 minutes

BAKE TIME
10 minutes

COOK TIME
5 minutes

1 can (10¾ ounces) Campbell's® Condensed Cream of Mushroom Soup (Regular *or* 98% Fat Free)
1 prepared pizza crust (12-inch)
1 tablespoon vegetable oil
3 cups frozen vegetables
⅛ teaspoon garlic powder
1 package (about 10 ounces) refrigerated cooked chicken strips
1 cup shredded Cheddar cheese (about 4 ounces)
Dried oregano leaves

1. Spread the soup on the crust to within ¼ inch of the edge. Bake at 450°F. for 5 minutes.

2. Heat the oil in a 10-inch skillet over medium heat. Add the vegetables and garlic powder and cook until the vegetables are tender-crisp, stirring occasionally.

3. Spoon the vegetables on the pizza. Top with the chicken and cheese. Sprinkle with the oregano, if desired.

4. Bake for 5 minutes or until the cheese is melted.

Easy Chicken & Cheese Enchiladas

Makes 6 servings

PREP TIME
15 minutes

BAKE TIME
40 minutes

1 **can (10¾ ounces) Campbell's® Condensed Cream of Chicken Soup (Regular *or* 98% Fat Free)**
½ **cup sour cream**
1 **cup Pace® Picante Sauce**
2 **teaspoons chili powder**
2 **cups chopped cooked chicken**
½ **cup shredded Monterey Jack cheese**
6 **flour tortillas (6-inch), warmed**
1 **small tomato, chopped (about ½ cup)**
1 **green onion, sliced (about 2 tablespoons)**

1. Heat the oven to 350°F. Stir the soup, sour cream, picante sauce and chili powder in a medium bowl.

2. Stir **1 cup** soup mixture, chicken and cheese in a large bowl.

3. Divide the chicken mixture among the tortillas. Roll up the tortillas and place seam-side up in a 2-quart shallow baking dish. Pour the remaining soup mixture over the filled tortillas. Cover the baking dish.

4. Bake for 40 minutes or until the enchiladas are hot and bubbling. Top with the tomato and onion.

Kitchen Tip

Stir ½ cup canned black beans, rinsed and drained, into the chicken mixture before filling the tortillas.

Chicken Crunch

Makes 4 servings

- **1 can (10¾ ounces) Campbell's® Condensed Cream of Chicken Soup (Regular *or* 98% Fat Free)**
- **½ cup milk**
- **4 skinless, boneless chicken breast halves (about 1 pound)**
- **2 tablespoons all-purpose flour**
- **1½ cups Pepperidge Farm® Herb Seasoned Stuffing, finely crushed**
- **2 tablespoons butter, melted**

PREP TIME
10 minutes

BAKE TIME
20 minutes

COOK TIME
5 minutes

1. Heat the oven to 400°F. Stir ⅓ **cup** soup and ¼ **cup** milk in a shallow dish. Coat the chicken with the flour. Dip the chicken in the soup mixture. Coat the chicken with the stuffing. Place the chicken onto a baking sheet. Drizzle with the butter.

2. Bake for 20 minutes or until the chicken is cooked through.

3. Heat the remaining soup and milk in a 1-quart saucepan over medium-high heat until the mixture is hot and bubbling. Serve the sauce with the chicken.

Turkey-Broccoli Twists

Makes 5 servings

PREP TIME
10 minutes

COOK TIME
20 minutes

- **3 cups *uncooked* corkscrew-shaped pasta**
- **2 cups broccoli florets**
- **2 medium carrots, sliced (about 1 cup)**
- **1 can (10¾ ounces) Campbell's® Condensed Cream of Broccoli Soup**
- **1¾ cups Swanson® Chicken Stock**
- **½ teaspoon garlic powder**
- **⅛ teaspoon ground black pepper**
- **2 cups cubed cooked turkey**
- **¼ cup grated Parmesan cheese**

1. Cook the pasta according to the package directions in a 3-quart saucepan, without salt. Add the broccoli and carrots for the last 5 minutes of the cooking time. Drain the pasta mixture well in a colander. Return the pasta mixture to the saucepan.

2. Stir the soup, stock, garlic powder, black pepper and turkey in the saucepan and cook over medium heat until the mixture is hot and bubbling. Sprinkle with the cheese.

Chicken Nachos

Makes 6 servings

½ cup Pace® Picante Sauce

1 can (10¾ ounces) Campbell's® Condensed Cheddar Cheese Soup

2 cans (4.5 ounces ***each***) Swanson® Premium White Chunk Chicken Breast in Water, drained

1 bag (about 10 ounces) tortilla chips

Chopped tomato

Sliced green onions

Sliced pitted ripe olives

1. Heat the picante sauce, soup and chicken in a 1-quart saucepan over medium heat until the mixture is hot and bubbling, stirring often.

2. Place the chips on a platter. Spoon the chicken mixture over the chips. Top with the tomato, onions and olives.

PREP TIME
10 minutes

COOK TIME
5 minutes

Tasty 2-Step Chicken Bake

Makes 4 servings

PREP TIME
5 minutes

BAKE TIME
25 minutes

4 skinless, boneless chicken breast halves (about 1 pound)

1 can (10¾ ounces) Campbell's® Condensed Cream of Mushroom Soup (Regular *or* 98% Fat Free)

1. Place the chicken into a 2-quart shallow baking dish. Spread the soup over the chicken. Cover the baking dish.

2. Bake at 400°F. for 25 minutes or until the chicken is cooked through.

Kitchen Tip

To prepare on top of the stove, brown the chicken in 1 tablespoon vegetable oil in a skillet. Stir in the soup and ½ cup water. Cover and cook for 5 minutes or until the chicken is cooked through.

Chicken Scampi

Makes 6 servings

- 2 tablespoons butter
- 6 skinless, boneless chicken breast halves (about 1½ pounds)
- 1 can (10¾ ounces) Campbell's® Condensed Cream of Chicken Soup (Regular ***or*** 98% Fat Free)
- ¼ cup water
- 2 teaspoons lemon juice
- 2 cloves garlic, minced
- Hot cooked pasta

PREP TIME
10 minutes

COOK TIME
20 minutes

1. Heat the butter in a 10-inch skillet over medium-high heat. Add the chicken and cook for 10 minutes or until well browned on both sides. Remove the chicken from the skillet.

2. Stir the soup, water, lemon juice and garlic in the skillet and heat to a boil. Return the chicken to the skillet. Reduce the heat to low. Cover and cook for 5 minutes or until the chicken is cooked through. Serve the chicken and sauce with the pasta.

Beef & Pork

Creamy Pork Marsala with Fettuccine

Makes 4 servings

PREP TIME
5 minutes

COOK TIME
25 minutes

Kitchen Tip

Marsalas can range from dry to sweet, so be sure to use a dry one for this recipe.

- **1 tablespoon olive oil**
- **4 boneless pork chops, ¾-inch thick (about 1 pound)**
- **1 cup sliced mushrooms (about 3 ounces)**
- **1 clove garlic, minced**
- **1 can (10¾ ounces) Campbell's® Condensed Cream of Mushroom Soup (Regular *or* 98% Fat Free)**
- **½ cup milk**
- **2 tablespoons dry Marsala wine**
- **8 ounces spinach fettuccine, cooked and drained**

1. Heat the oil in a 10-inch skillet over medium-high heat. Add the pork and cook until well browned on both sides.

2. Reduce the heat to medium. Add the mushrooms and garlic to the skillet and cook until the mushrooms are tender.

3. Stir the soup, milk and wine in the skillet and heat to a boil. Reduce the heat to low. Cover and cook for 5 minutes or until the pork is cooked through. Serve the pork and sauce with the pasta.

Zesty Pork Chops

Makes 4 servings

PREP TIME
5 minutes

COOK TIME
30 minutes

Kitchen Tip

You can really spice up this recipe by adding 1 teaspoon hot pepper sauce to the picante sauce mixture.

4 bone-in pork chops (about 1¼ pounds)
All-purpose flour
1 cup Pace® Picante Sauce
2 tablespoons packed brown sugar
1 apple, peeled and cut into ¼-inch-thick slices
2 tablespoons olive oil

1. Coat the pork with the flour. Stir the picante sauce, brown sugar and apple in a medium bowl.

2. Heat the oil in a 10-inch skillet over medium-high heat. Add the pork and cook until well browned on both sides. Pour off any fat.

3. Pour the picante sauce mixture over the pork. Reduce the heat to low. Cover and cook for 20 minutes or until the pork is cooked through.

Bistro Onion Burgers

Makes 6 servings

1½ pounds ground beef
1 envelope (about 1 ounce) dry onion soup and recipe mix
3 tablespoons water
6 Pepperidge Farm® Classic Sandwich Buns with Sesame Seeds, split and toasted
Lettuce leaves
Tomato slices

1. Thoroughly mix the beef, soup mix and water. Shape the beef mixture into **6** (½-inch-thick) burgers.

2. Cook the burgers in batches in a 10-inch skillet over medium-high heat until well browned on both sides, 10 minutes for medium or to desired doneness.

3. Serve the burgers on the buns. Top with the lettuce and tomato.

PREP TIME
5 minutes

COOK TIME
10 minutes

Steak with Chipotle Cheese Sauce

Makes 8 servings

PREP TIME
20 minutes

COOK TIME
10 minutes

GRILL TIME
15 minutes

- **1 tablespoon olive oil**
- **2 large white onions *or* 1 large sweet onion, coarsely chopped (about 2 cups)**
- **1 can (10¾ ounces) Campbell's® Condensed Cheddar Cheese Soup**
- **½ cup milk**
- **½ teaspoon ground chipotle chile pepper**
- **2 medium tomatoes, coarsely chopped (about 2 cups)**
- **1 skirt *or* beef flank steak (about 2 pounds), 1-inch thick, cut into 8 pieces**
- **¼ cup chopped fresh cilantro leaves (optional)**

1. Heat the oil in a 2-quart saucepan over medium heat. Add the onions and cook for 5 minutes or until tender, stirring occasionally.

2. Stir the soup, milk, chipotle chile pepper and tomatoes in the saucepan. Reduce the heat to low. Cook and stir for 3 minutes or until the mixture is hot and bubbling, stirring occasionally.

3. Lightly oil the grill rack and heat the grill to medium. Grill the beef for 15 minutes for medium or to desired doneness, turning the beef over once halfway through the grilling time. Spoon the soup mixture over the beef and sprinkle with the cilantro, if desired.

Baked Potatoes Olé

Makes 4 servings

- 1 pound ground beef
- 1 tablespoon chili powder
- 1 cup Pace® Picante Sauce
- 4 hot baked potatoes, split
- Shredded Cheddar cheese

1. Cook the beef and chili powder in a 10-inch skillet over medium-high heat until the beef is well browned, stirring often to separate the meat. Pour off any fat.

2. Stir the picante sauce in the skillet. Reduce the heat to low. Cook until the mixture is hot and bubbling. Serve the beef mixture over the potatoes. Top with the cheese.

PREP TIME
5 minutes

COOK TIME
15 minutes

Kitchen Tip

To bake the potatoes, pierce the potatoes with a fork. Bake at 400°F. for 1 hour or microwave on HIGH for 12 minutes or until fork-tender.

Pork Tenderloin with Peach & Pecan Sauce

Makes 4 servings

PREP TIME
20 minutes

COOK TIME
20 minutes

- **1 tablespoon olive oil**
- **1 pork tenderloin (about 1 pound), cut into ¾-inch-thick slices**
- **2 cloves garlic, minced**
- **2 green onions, sliced (about ¼ cup)**
- **1 can (10¾ ounces) Campbell's® Condensed Golden Mushroom Soup**
- **1 can (about 15 ounces) sliced peaches in juice, drained, reserving juice**
- **3 tablespoons low-sodium soy sauce**
- **2 tablespoons honey**
- **¼ cup pecan halves, toasted and broken into large pieces**
- **Hot cooked rice**

1. Heat the oil in a 10-inch skillet over medium-high heat. Add the pork and cook until well browned on both sides. Remove the pork from the skillet.

2. Add the garlic and onions to the skillet and cook and stir for 1 minute. Stir the soup, peach juice, soy sauce and honey in the skillet and heat to a boil. Cook for 5 minutes or until the soup mixture is slightly reduced.

3. Return the pork to the skillet. Stir in the peaches. Reduce the heat to low. Cook until the pork is cooked through. Stir in the pecans. Serve the pork and sauce with the rice. Sprinkle with additional sliced green onion, if desired.

Tasty 2-Step Pork Chops

Makes 4 servings

- **1 tablespoon vegetable oil**
- **4 bone-in pork chops, ½-inch thick (about 1½ pounds)**
- **1 can (10¾ ounces) Campbell's® Condensed Cream of Mushroom Soup (Regular *or* 98% Fat Free)**
- **½ cup water**

1. Heat the oil in a 10-inch skillet over medium-high heat. Add the pork and cook until well browned on both sides.

2. Stir the soup and water in the skillet and heat to a boil. Reduce the heat to low. Cover and cook for 10 minutes or until the pork is cooked through.

Garlic Pork Chops: Add **1** clove garlic, minced, to the skillet with the pork chops.

PREP TIME
5 minutes

COOK TIME
20 minutes

Kitchen Tip

Also great with Campbell's® Condensed Cream of Mushroom with Roasted Garlic Soup, with ½ cup milk instead of water.

Chipotle Pork Taco Cups

Makes 10 servings

PREP TIME
15 minutes

BAKE TIME
5 minutes

COOK TIME
5 minutes

Vegetable cooking spray
10 whole wheat *or* flour tortillas (6-inch)
1 container (18 ounces) refrigerated cooked barbecue sauce with shredded pork (about 2 cups)
1 cup Pace® Picante Sauce
¼ teaspoon ground chipotle chile pepper
Shredded Cheddar cheese (optional)
Guacamole (optional)
Sour cream (optional)
Sliced ripe olives (optional)

1. Heat the oven to 350°F. Spray **10** (3-inch) muffin-pan cups with the cooking spray.

2. Wrap the tortillas between damp paper towels. Microwave on HIGH for 30 seconds or until the tortillas are warm. Fold **1** tortilla into thirds to form a cone shape. Press the tortilla cone, wide end down, into a muffin-pan cup. Repeat with the remaining tortillas, rewarming in the microwave as needed.

3. Bake for 5 minutes or until the tortilla cones are golden. Remove the tortillas from the pan and cool on wire racks.

4. Heat the pork, picante sauce and chipotle chile pepper in a 2-quart saucepan over medium heat until the mixture is hot and bubbling, stirring often.

5. Spoon **about ¼ cup** pork mixture into **each** tortilla cone. Top with the cheese, guacamole, sour cream or olives, if desired.

Kitchen Tip

You can prepare the tortillas through the baking step up to 24 hours ahead of time and store them in an airtight container.

Soft Tacos

Makes 8 servings

- **1 pound ground beef**
- **1 tablespoon chili powder**
- **1 cup Pace® Picante Sauce**
- **8 flour tortillas (8-inch), warmed**
- **1 cup shredded lettuce**
- **1 cup shredded Cheddar cheese**

1. Cook beef and chili powder in a 10-inch skillet over medium-high heat until the beef is well browned, stirring often to separate the meat. Pour off any fat.

2. Stir the picante sauce in the skillet and cook until the mixture is hot and bubbling.

3. Spoon **about ¼ cup** beef mixture down the center of **each** tortilla. Top with the lettuce and cheese. Fold the tortillas around the filling. Serve with additional picante sauce.

PREP TIME
10 minutes

COOK TIME
15 minutes

Orange Beef Steak

Makes 6 servings

PREP TIME
10 minutes

COOK TIME
25 minutes

- **1 jar (12 ounces) Campbell's® Slow Roast Beef Gravy**
- **1 tablespoon grated orange zest**
- **2 tablespoons orange juice**
- **½ teaspoon garlic powder *or* 2 cloves garlic, minced**
- **1 boneless beef top round steak, 1½-inch thick (about 1½ pounds)**

1. Stir the gravy, orange zest, orange juice and garlic powder in a 1-quart saucepan.

2. Heat the broiler. Place the beef on a rack in a broiler pan. Broil 4 inches from the heat for 25 minutes for medium or to desired doneness, turning the beef over halfway through cooking and brushing often with the gravy mixture. Thinly slice the beef.

3. Heat the remaining gravy mixture over medium-high heat to a boil. Serve the gravy mixture with the beef.

Super Easy Baked Pork Chops

Makes 6 servings

6 pork chops, ¾-inch thick (about 2 pounds)

1 jar (24 ounces) Prego® Fresh Mushroom Italian Sauce

6 cups medium tube-shaped pasta (ziti) or spaghetti, cooked and drained

1. Heat the oven to 400°F. Arrange the chops in a 3-quart shallow baking dish. Bake for 20 minutes.

2. Pour the Italian sauce over the chops. Bake for 15 minutes or until chops are cooked through. Stir the sauce before serving. Serve with the pasta.

PREP TIME
5 minutes

BAKE TIME
35 minutes

Buffalo Burgers

Makes 4 servings

PREP TIME
10 minutes

GRILL TIME
10 minutes

COOK TIME
10 minutes

- **1 pound ground beef**
- **1 can (10¾ ounces) Campbell's® Condensed Tomato Soup (Regular *or* Healthy Request®)**
- **½ teaspoon Louisiana-style hot sauce**
- **½ cup crumbled blue cheese *or* 4 slices blue cheese**
- **4 Pepperidge Farm® Classic Sandwich Buns with Sesame Seeds, split**
- **Lettuce leaves, red onion slices, tomato slices (optional)**

1. Shape the beef into **4** (½-inch-thick) burgers.

2. Lightly oil the grill rack and heat the grill to medium. Grill the burgers for 10 minutes for medium or to desired doneness, turning the burgers over once halfway through grilling time.

3. Heat the soup and hot sauce in a 1-quart saucepan over medium heat to a boil. Reduce the heat to low. Cover and cook for 5 minutes. Top the burgers with the soup mixture. Sprinkle with the cheese. Serve the burgers on the buns with the lettuce, onion and tomato, if desired.

Kitchen Tip

Any leftover soup mixture can also be a great dipping sauce for French fries.

Shortcut Stuffed Peppers

Makes 4 servings

- 1½ pounds ground beef
- 1 can (10¾ ounces) Campbell's® Condensed Tomato Soup
- 1 cup ***uncooked*** instant white rice
- 2 teaspoons garlic powder
- ½ teaspoon ground black pepper
- 2 large green peppers, cut in half lengthwise and seeded

PREP TIME
10 minutes

COOK TIME
10 minutes

1. Mix the beef, soup, rice, garlic powder and black pepper in a large bowl.

2. Place the pepper halves, cut-side up, into an 8×8-inch microwavable baking dish. Divide the beef mixture among the pepper halves (the pepper halves will be very full).

3. Cover and microwave on HIGH for 10 minutes or until the beef mixture is cooked through.

Mushroom-Smothered Beef Burgers

Makes 4 servings

PREP TIME
15 minutes

COOK TIME
25 minutes

Kitchen Tip

You can substitute ground turkey for the ground beef in this recipe.

- **1 can (10¾ ounces) Campbell's® Condensed Cream of Mushroom Soup (Regular *or* 98% Fat Free)**
- **1 pound ground beef**
- **⅓ cup Italian-seasoned dry bread crumbs**
- **1 small onion, finely chopped (about ¼ cup)**
- **1 egg, beaten**
- **1 tablespoon vegetable oil**
- **1 tablespoon Worcestershire sauce**
- **2 tablespoons water**
- **1½ cups sliced mushrooms (about 4 ounces)**

1. Thoroughly mix **¼ cup** soup, beef, bread crumbs, onion and egg in a large bowl. Shape the beef mixture firmly into **4** (½-inch-thick) burgers.

2. Heat the oil in a 10-inch skillet over medium-high heat. Add the burgers and cook until they're well browned on both sides. Pour off any fat.

3. Add the remaining soup, Worcestershire, water and mushrooms to the skillet and heat to a boil. Reduce the heat to low. Cover and cook for 10 minutes or until the burgers are cooked through.

Quick Spaghetti & Meatballs

Makes 6 servings

- **1 jar (45 ounces) Prego® Flavored with Meat Italian Sauce**
- **16 frozen meatballs (1 ounce *each*)**
- **1 package (1 pound) spaghetti, cooked and drained (about 8 cups)**
- **Grated Parmesan cheese**

1. Stir the Italian sauce and meatballs in a 3-quart saucepan and heat to a boil over medium heat. Reduce the heat to low. Cover and cook for 20 minutes or until the meatballs are heated through, stirring occasionally.

2. Serve the sauce and meatballs over the spaghetti. Sprinkle with the cheese.

PREP TIME
5 minutes

COOK TIME
25 minutes

Gridiron Cheddar & Garlic Steak Fajitas

Makes 6 servings

PREP TIME
15 minutes

COOK TIME
15 minutes

1 tablespoon olive oil
2 large red, orange *or* yellow peppers, cut into 2-inch-long strips (about 4 cups)
1 large onion, thinly sliced (about 1 cup)
2 cloves garlic, minced
1 skirt *or* boneless beef sirloin steak, ¾ inches thick (about 1½ pounds), cut into very thin strips
1 can (10¾ ounces) Campbell's® Condensed Cheddar Cheese Soup
1 tablespoon lime juice
6 flour tortillas (8-inch), warmed
1 jar (16 ounces) Pace® Picante Sauce
***Toppings:* Shredded Cheddar cheese, chopped avocado, hot pepper sauce, sour cream *and* shredded lettuce**
Lime wedges

1. Heat the oil in a deep 12-inch skillet over medium-high heat. Add the peppers and onion and cook until the vegetables are tender, stirring occasionally. Add the garlic and cook and stir for 30 seconds. Remove the vegetable mixture from the skillet.

2. Add the beef and cook until well browned, stirring often. Remove the beef from the skillet.

3. Stir the soup and lime juice in the skillet and heat to a boil. Return the vegetables and beef to the skillet and cook until the mixture is hot and bubbling.

4. Spoon **about ¼ cup** beef mixture down the center of **each** tortilla. Top with the picante sauce and toppings, if desired. Wrap the tortillas around the filling. Serve with the lime wedges, if desired.

Kitchen Tip

Substitute warmed taco shells for the flour tortillas.

Steak with Tomato Gorgonzola Sauce

Makes 6 servings

PREP TIME
10 minutes

COOK TIME
25 minutes

- **Vegetable cooking spray**
- **1 boneless beef sirloin steak *or* top round steak, ¾-inch thick, thinly sliced (about 1½ pounds)**
- **1 package (8 ounces) sliced mushrooms**
- **1 large onion, thinly sliced (about 1 cup)**
- **¼ cup balsamic vinegar**
- **1 cup Prego® Traditional Italian Sauce *or* Marinara Italian Sauce**
- **½ cup crumbled gorgonzola *or* feta cheese**
- **Hot mashed potatoes**

1. Spray a 12-inch skillet with the cooking spray and heat over medium-high heat for 1 minute. Add the beef in 2 batches and cook until well browned, stirring often. Remove the beef from the skillet. Pour off any fat.

2. Reduce the heat to medium. Add the mushrooms and onion to the skillet and cook for 5 minutes or until the vegetables are tender. Stir in the vinegar and cook for 2 minutes.

3. Stir the Italian sauce in the skillet and heat to a boil. Return the beef to the skillet. Top with the cheese. Cook and stir until the cheese is melted. Serve with the potatoes.

Polynesian Burgers

Makes 6 servings

1½	pounds ground beef
1	can (8 ounces) pineapple slices in juice, undrained
1	can (10½ ounces) Campbell's® Condensed French Onion Soup
2	teaspoons packed brown sugar
1	tablespoon cider vinegar
1	loaf French bread, cut crosswise into 6 pieces

PREP TIME
10 minutes

COOK TIME
20 minutes

1. Shape the beef into **6** (½-inch-thick) burgers.

2. Cook the burgers in a 12-inch skillet over medium-high heat until well browned on both sides. Pour off any fat. Top **each** burger with **1** slice pineapple. Reserve the pineapple juice.

3. Stir the soup, reserved pineapple juice, brown sugar and vinegar in a small bowl. Add the soup mixture to the skillet and heat to a boil. Reduce the heat to low. Cover and cook for 5 minutes or until the burgers are cooked through.

4. Split the bread pieces. Serve the burgers and sauce on the bread.

Pork with Mushroom Dijon Sauce

Makes 4 servings

PREP TIME
10 minutes

COOK TIME
30 minutes

- **4 boneless pork chops, ¾-inch thick (about 1 pound)**
- **½ teaspoon lemon pepper seasoning**
- **1 tablespoon vegetable oil**
- **1 cup sliced mushrooms (about 3 ounces)**
- **1 can (10¾ ounces) Campbell's® Condensed Cream of Mushroom Soup (Regular *or* 98% Fat Free)**
- **¼ cup milk**
- **2 tablespoons Chablis *or* other dry white wine**
- **1 tablespoon Dijon-style mustard**

1. Season the pork with the lemon pepper.

2. Heat the oil in a 10-inch skillet over medium-high heat. Add the pork and cook until well browned on both sides. Remove the pork from the skillet.

3. Add the mushrooms to the skillet. Reduce the heat to medium. Cook until the mushrooms are tender, stirring occasionally.

4. Stir the soup, milk, wine and mustard in the skillet and heat to a boil. Return the pork to the skillet. Reduce the heat to low. Cover and cook for 10 minutes or until the pork is cooked through.

Shortcut Ravioli Lasagna

Makes 6 servings

PREP TIME
10 minutes

BAKE TIME
45 minutes

STAND TIME
10 minutes

- **Vegetable cooking spray**
- **3 cups Prego® Italian Sausage & Garlic Italian Sauce**
- **½ cup water**
- **1 package (30 ounces) frozen regular-size cheese-filled ravioli (about 30 to 34)**
- **6 ounces shredded mozzarella cheese (about 1½ cups)**
- **Grated Parmesan cheese *and* chopped fresh parsley for garnish**

1. Heat the oven to 375°F. Spray a 13×9×2-inch baking dish with cooking spray.

2. Stir the Italian sauce and water in a large bowl. Spread **1 cup** of the sauce mixture in the baking dish. Top with ½ of the ravioli, **¾ cup** mozzarella cheese and **1 cup** sauce mixture. Top with the remaining ravioli and sauce mixture. Cover the baking dish.

3. Bake for 35 minutes or until the mixture is hot and bubbling. Uncover the baking dish. Sprinkle with the remaining mozzarella cheese.

4. Bake for 10 minutes or until the cheese is melted. Let stand for 10 minutes. Garnish with the Parmesan cheese and parsley.

Sensational Sides

Country Scalloped Potatoes

Makes 6 servings

PREP TIME
15 minutes

BAKE TIME
1 hour 10 minutes

STAND TIME
10 minutes

- **1 can (10¾ ounces) Campbell's® Condensed Cream of Celery Soup (Regular *or* 98% Fat Free)**
- **1 can (10½ ounces) Campbell's® Chicken Gravy**
- **1 cup milk**
- **5 medium potatoes, peeled and thinly sliced (about 5 cups)**
- **1 small onion, thinly sliced (about ¼ cup)**
- **2½ cups diced cooked ham**
- **1 cup shredded Cheddar cheese (about 4 ounces)**

1. Stir the soup, gravy and milk in a small bowl. Layer **half** the potatoes, onion, ham and soup mixture in a 3-quart shallow baking dish. Repeat the layers. Cover the baking dish.

2. Bake at 375°F. for 40 minutes. Uncover and bake for 25 minutes. Top with the cheese. Bake for 5 minutes or until the potatoes are tender and the cheese is melted. Let stand for 10 minutes.

Cheddar Potato Casserole

Makes 8 servings

PREP TIME
10 minutes

BAKE TIME
30 minutes

3 cups prepared mashed potatoes

1 can (10¾ ounces) Campbell's® Condensed Cheddar Cheese Soup

⅓ cup sour cream *or* yogurt

Generous dash ground black pepper

1 green onion, chopped (about 2 tablespoons)

1. Stir the potatoes, soup, sour cream, black pepper and onion in a medium bowl. Spoon the potato mixture into a 1½-quart baking dish.

2. Bake at 350°F. for 30 minutes or until the potato mixture is hot.

Kitchen Tip

To make 3 cups mashed potatoes, place 2 pounds potatoes, peeled and cut into 1-inch pieces, into a 3-quart saucepan. Add water to cover and heat over medium-high heat to a boil. Reduce the heat to low. Cover and cook for 10 minutes or until the potatoes are tender. Drain. Mash the potatoes with ¾ cup milk and 2 tablespoons butter.

Bulgur Salad

Makes 6 servings

- **1¼ cups water**
- **1 cup *uncooked* bulgur wheat**
- **1 cup Pace® Pico De Gallo *or* Pace® Picante Sauce**
- **1 cup rinsed, drained canned black beans**
- **1 cup drained canned whole kernel corn**
- **¼ cup chopped fresh cilantro leaves**

1. Heat the water in a 2-quart saucepan over medium-high heat to a boil. Stir the bulgur into the saucepan. Remove the saucepan from the heat. Let stand for 20 minutes.

2. Stir the bulgur, pico de gallo, beans, corn and cilantro in a medium bowl. Serve immediately or cover and refrigerate until ready to serve.

PREP TIME
10 minutes

COOK TIME
5 minutes

STAND TIME
20 minutes

Kitchen Tip

For a twist, stir in a squeeze of fresh lime juice.

Green Bean Casserole

Makes 12 servings

PREP TIME
10 minutes

BAKE TIME
30 minutes

Kitchen Tip

Use 2 bags (16 to 20 ounces each) frozen green beans, 4 packages (9 ounces each) frozen green beans, 4 cans (about 16 ounces each) green beans or about 3 pounds fresh green beans for this recipe.

- **2 cans (10¾ ounces *each*) Campbell's® Condensed Cream of Mushroom Soup (Regular *or* 98% Fat Free)**
- **1 cup milk**
- **2 teaspoons soy sauce**
- **¼ teaspoon ground black pepper**
- **8 cups cooked cut green beans**
- **2⅔ cups French fried onions**

1. Stir the soup, milk, soy sauce, black pepper, beans and **1⅓ cups** onions in a 3-quart casserole.

2. Bake at 350°F. for 25 minutes or until the bean mixture is hot and bubbling. Stir the bean mixture. Sprinkle with the remaining onions.

3. Bake for 5 minutes or until the onions are golden brown.

Add crunch: Add ½ **cup** sliced almonds to the onion topping.

Bacon lovers: Add **4** slices bacon, cooked and crumbled, to the bean mixture.

Add a festive touch: Add ½ **cup** chopped red pepper with the soup.

Cheese lovers: Stir in **1 cup** shredded Cheddar cheese with the soup. Omit soy sauce. Sprinkle with an additional ½ **cup** Cheddar cheese when adding the remaining onions.

Golden Green Bean Casserole: Substitute Campbell's® Condensed Golden Mushroom Soup for the Cream of Mushroom Soup. Omit soy sauce. Stir in ½ **cup** chopped red pepper with the green beans.

Tuscan Bread Salad

Makes 2 servings

- **¼ cup prepared fat-free red wine vinaigrette dressing**
- **1 cup Pepperidge Farm® Whole Grain Seasoned Croutons**
- **2 medium tomatoes, diced (about 2 cups)**
- **½ cup cubed fresh mozzarella cheese**
- **2 green onions, thinly sliced (about ¼ cup)**
- **6 fresh basil leaves, cut into thin strips *or* torn into small pieces**

Pour the dressing into a medium bowl. Add the croutons, tomatoes, cheese, onions and basil and toss to coat.

PREP TIME
10 minutes

Caramelized Onion with Pancetta & Rosemary Stuffing

Makes 12 servings

PREP TIME
20 minutes

COOK TIME
30 minutes

BAKE TIME
30 minutes

- **6 tablespoons butter**
- **2 large sweet onions, diced (about 3 cups)**
- **1 package (4 ounces) cubed pancetta (about 1 cup)**
- **4 cloves garlic, chopped**
- **2 stalks celery, diced (about 1 cup)**
- **2 tablespoons chopped fresh rosemary leaves**
- **3 cups Swanson® Chicken Broth (Regular, Natural Goodness® *or* Certified Organic)**
- **¼ cup sherry**
- **1 package (14 ounces) Pepperidge Farm® Herb Seasoned Stuffing**

1. Heat the oven to 350°F.

2. Heat the butter in a 3-quart saucepan over medium heat. Add the onions and cook for 15 minutes or until well browned, stirring occasionally.

3. Stir the pancetta, garlic, celery and rosemary in the saucepan and cook until the pancetta is well browned, stirring occasionally. Stir in the broth and sherry and heat to a boil. Remove the saucepan from the heat. Add the stuffing and mix lightly. Spoon the stuffing mixture into a greased 3-quart casserole. Cover the casserole.

4. Bake for 30 minutes or until the stuffing mixture is hot.

Baked Corn Casserole

Makes 6 servings

1 can (10¾ ounces) Campbell's® Condensed Cream of Chicken Soup (Regular *or* 98% Fat Free)

½ cup milk

2 eggs

1 can (about 16 ounces) whole kernel corn, drained

1 package (about 8 ounces) corn muffin mix

¼ cup grated Parmesan cheese

1 can (2.8 ounces) French fried onions (about 1⅓ cups)

1. Beat the soup, milk and eggs in a medium bowl with a fork or whisk. Stir in the corn, corn muffin mix, cheese and **⅔ cup** onions. Pour the soup mixture into a 1½-quart casserole.

2. Bake at 350°F. for 30 minutes or until the mixture is hot.

3. Top with the remaining onions. Bake for 5 minutes or until the onions are golden brown.

PREP TIME
10 minutes

BAKE TIME
35 minutes

Moist & Savory Stuffing

Makes 10 servings

PREP TIME
10 minutes

COOK TIME
10 minutes

BAKE TIME
30 minutes

Kitchen Tip

For crunchier stuffing, bake the casserole uncovered.

2½ cups Swanson® Chicken Broth (Regular, Natural Goodness® *or* Certified Organic)
Generous dash ground black pepper
2 stalks celery, coarsely chopped (about 1 cup)
1 large onion, coarsely chopped (about 1 cup)
1 package (16 ounces) Pepperidge Farm® Herb Seasoned Stuffing

1. Heat the broth, black pepper, celery and onion in a 3-quart saucepan over medium-high heat to a boil. Reduce the heat to low. Cover and cook for 5 minutes or until the vegetables are tender, stirring often. Remove the saucepan from the heat. Add the stuffing and mix lightly.

2. Spoon the stuffing mixture into a greased 3-quart shallow baking dish. Cover the baking dish.

3. Bake at 350°F. for 30 minutes or until the stuffing is hot.

Cranberry & Pecan Stuffing: Stir ½ **cup each** dried cranberries and chopped pecans into the stuffing mixture before baking.

Sausage & Mushroom Stuffing: Add **1 cup** sliced mushrooms to the vegetables during cooking. Stir ½ **pound** pork sausage, cooked and crumbled, into the stuffing mixture before baking.

Glazed Snow Peas and Carrots

Makes 6 servings

4 teaspoons cornstarch

1¾ cups Swanson® Chicken Broth (Regular, Natural Goodness® *or* Certified Organic)

1 teaspoon lemon juice

4 medium carrots, sliced (about 2 cups)

1 medium onion, chopped (about ½ cup)

8 ounces snow peas (about 2 cups)

1. Stir the cornstarch, **½ cup** broth and lemon juice in a small bowl until the mixture is smooth.

2. Stir the remaining broth, carrots and onion in the skillet and heat to a boil. Reduce the heat to low. Cover and cook for 5 minutes or until the vegetables are tender. Stir in the snow peas and cook for 2 minutes.

3. Stir the cornstarch mixture in the skillet. Cook until the mixture boils and thickens.

PREP TIME
10 minutes

COOK TIME
20 minutes

Kitchen Tip

For a meatless version, substitute Swanson® Vegetable Broth for the chicken broth.

Cheesy Chile Corn Casserole

Makes 6 servings

PREP TIME
15 minutes

BAKE TIME
30 minutes

Kitchen Tip

An oven thermometer is the best way to check the accuracy of your oven. Most are designed to hang inside your oven on the rack and can measure temperatures from 100°F. to 600°F.

- **1 can (10¾ ounces) Campbell's® Condensed Cheddar Cheese Soup**
- **¼ cup milk**
- **1 tablespoon butter, melted**
- **Dash ground red pepper**
- **1 bag (16 ounces) frozen whole kernel corn, thawed**
- **1 can (4.5 ounces) chopped green chiles**
- **1 can (2.8 ounces) French fried onions (about 1⅓ cups)**

1. Heat the oven to 350°F. Stir the soup, milk, butter, pepper, corn, chiles and **⅔ cup** onions in a 1½-quart casserole.

2. Bake for 25 minutes or until the corn mixture is hot and bubbling. Stir the corn mixture. Sprinkle the remaining onions over the corn mixture.

3. Bake for 5 minutes or until the onions are golden brown.

BLT Salad Toss

Makes 6 servings

- ½ cup Pace® Picante Sauce
- ¼ cup prepared Italian salad dressing
- 6 cups romaine lettuce, torn into bite-sized pieces
- 2 medium tomatoes, cut into thin wedges
- ⅔ cup sliced pitted ripe olives
- 2 cups corn chips
- 2 ounces shredded Cheddar cheese (about ½ cup)
- 3 slices bacon, cooked and crumbled

1. Stir the picante sauce and dressing in a large bowl.

2. Add the lettuce, tomatoes, olives and chips and toss to coat. Top with the cheese and bacon. Serve immediately.

PREP TIME
20 minutes

Cheesy Mushroom Potato Topper

Makes 4 servings

PREP TIME
10 minutes

COOK TIME
4 minutes

Generous dash ground black pepper

1 can (10¾ ounces) Campbell's® Condensed Cream of Mushroom Soup (Regular *or* 98% Fat Free)

4 hot baked potatoes, split

¼ cup shredded Cheddar cheese

1. Add the black pepper to the soup in the can and stir until the soup is smooth.

2. Place the potatoes onto a microwavable plate. Spoon the soup on the potatoes. Sprinkle with the cheese.

3. Microwave on HIGH for 4 minutes or until the soup mixture is hot and the cheese is melted.

Kitchen Tip

To bake the potatoes, pierce the potatoes with a fork. Microwave on HIGH for 10 minutes or bake at 400°F. for 1 hour or until fork-tender.

Layered Tex-Mex Salad

Makes 8 servings

- ½ cup Pace® Picante Sauce
- ½ cup mayonnaise
- ¼ cup sour cream ***or*** plain yogurt
- 3 cups coarsely shredded lettuce
- 2 medium tomatoes, chopped (about 2 cups)
- 1 small cucumber, cut in half lengthwise and sliced (about 1½ cups)
- 1 medium red onion, sliced
- 1 large avocado, peeled, pitted and thinly sliced (about 1 cup)
- ¼ cup sliced pitted ripe olives

1. Stir the picante sauce, mayonnaise and sour cream in a small bowl.

2. Layer the lettuce, tomatoes, cucumber, onion and avocado in a large clear glass bowl. Spoon the picante sauce mixture over the top. Sprinkle with the olives. Serve immediately.

PREP TIME
20 minutes

Sausage Walnut Stuffing

Makes 12 servings

PREP TIME
10 minutes

COOK TIME
15 minutes

- **½ pound bulk pork sausage**
- **¼ cup (½ stick) butter**
- **2 stalks celery, sliced (about 1 cup)**
- **1 large onion, chopped (about 1 cup)**
- **1 medium apple, cored and chopped**
- **1¾ cups Swanson® Chicken Broth (Regular, Natural Goodness® *or* Certified Organic)**
- **1 bag (14 ounces) Pepperidge Farm® Cubed Country Style Stuffing**
- **½ cup chopped walnuts**

1. Cook the sausage in a 4-quart saucepot until well browned. Pour off any fat. Add the butter, celery, onion and apple and cook until tender.

2. Add the broth and heat to a boil. Remove the saucepot from the heat. Add the stuffing and walnuts. Mix lightly.

Mexican Corn Casserole

Makes 6 servings

Vegetable cooking spray

1 can (10¾ ounces) Campbell's® Condensed Cheddar Cheese Soup

1 cup Pace® Picante Sauce

1 bag (16 ounces) frozen whole kernel corn, thawed

1 cup coarsely crushed tortilla chips

1. Spray a 2-quart casserole with the cooking spray. Stir the soup, picante sauce and corn in the casserole. Sprinkle with the tortilla chips.

2. Bake at 350°F. for 30 minutes or until the mixture is hot and bubbling.

PREP TIME
5 minutes

BAKE TIME
30 minutes

Glazed Vegetables

Makes 4 servings

PREP TIME
20 minutes

COOK TIME
10 minutes

- **2 tablespoons cornstarch**
- **1¾ cups Swanson® Vegetable Broth (Regular *or* Certified Organic)**
- **½ teaspoon ground ginger**
- **¼ teaspoon garlic powder *or* 1 clove garlic, minced**
- **2 medium carrots, sliced (about 1 cup)**
- **2 stalks celery, sliced (about 1 cup)**
- **1 small red *or* green pepper, cut into 2-inch-long strips (about 1 cup)**
- **1 large onion, cut into wedges**
- **1 cup fresh *or* frozen broccoli florets**
- **4 ounces snow peas**

1. Stir the cornstarch and ¼ **cup** broth in a small bowl until the mixture is smooth.

2. Stir the remaining broth, ginger, garlic powder, carrots, celery, pepper, onion, broccoli and snow peas in a 10-inch skillet and heat to a boil over medium-high heat. Reduce the heat to medium. Cover the skillet and cook for 5 minutes or until the vegetables are tender-crisp.

3. Stir the cornstarch mixture into the skillet. Cook and stir until the mixture boils and thickens.

Harvest Salad

Makes 8 servings

PREP TIME
10 minutes

- **2 packages (about 7 ounces *each*) mixed salad greens (about 8 cups)**
- **2 cups cut-up fresh vegetables (red onions, cucumbers *and* carrots)**
- **1 can (10¾ ounces) Campbell's® Condensed Tomato Soup (Regular *or* Healthy Request®)**
- **¼ cup vegetable oil**
- **¼ cup red wine vinegar**
- **1 tablespoon honey *or* sugar**
- **1 package (0.7 ounce) Italian salad dressing mix**
- **2 cups your favorite Pepperidge Farm® croutons**
- **¼ cup shelled pumpkin *or* sunflower seeds**

1. Place the salad greens and vegetables into a large bowl.

2. Beat the soup, oil, vinegar, honey and salad dressing mix in a small bowl with a fork or whisk. Pour **¾ cup** soup mixture over the salad mixture and toss to coat.

3. Arrange the salad on a serving platter. Top with the croutons and pumpkin seeds. Serve the salad with the remaining soup mixture.

New Potatoes and Peas

Makes 7 servings

PREP TIME
10 minutes

COOK TIME
20 minutes

- **9 small new potatoes, cut into quarters (about 1½ pounds)**
- **1 can (10¾ ounces) Campbell's® Condensed Cream of Mushroom Soup (Regular *or* 98% Fat Free)**
- **⅓ cup milk**
- **½ teaspoon dried thyme leaves *or* dill weed, crushed**
- **⅛ teaspoon ground black pepper**
- **1 package (10 ounces) frozen peas *or* peas with pearl onions, thawed and drained**

1. Place the potatoes in a 4-quart saucepan. Cover the potatoes with water. Heat over high heat to a boil. Reduce the heat to medium. Cook for 8 minutes or until the potatoes are fork-tender. Drain the potatoes in a colander.

2. In the same saucepan, stir the soup, milk, thyme and black pepper. Stir in the potatoes and peas. Heat over low heat, stirring occasionally until heated through.

Savory Vegetables

Makes 4 servings

1 cup Swanson® Chicken Broth (Regular, Natural Goodness® *or* Certified Organic)

3 cups cut-up vegetables*

Use a combination of broccoli florets, cauliflower florets, sliced carrots and sliced celery.

1. Heat the broth and vegetables in a 3-quart saucepan over medium-high heat to a boil.

2. Reduce the heat to low. Cover and cook for 5 minutes or until the vegetables are tender-crisp. Drain the vegetables.

PREP TIME
5 minutes

COOK TIME
10 minutes

Desserts

Lemon Cheesecake Mini Tartlets

Makes 36 tartlets

THAW TIME
40 minutes

PREP TIME
20 minutes

BAKE TIME
10 minutes

COOL TIME
20 minutes

CHILL TIME
10 minutes

Kitchen Tip

To make ahead, prepare as directed above. Cover and refrigerate for up to 24 hours.

- ½ **of a 17.3-ounce package Pepperidge Farm® Puff Pastry Sheets (1 sheet), thawed**
- **1 egg, beaten**
- ½ **of an 8-ounce package cream cheese, softened**
- ½ **cup prepared lemon curd**
- ½ **cup thawed frozen whipped topping**
- **Fresh raspberries *or* blueberries**

1. Heat the oven to 375°F. Lightly grease **36** (1½-inch) mini muffin-pan cups.

2. Unfold the pastry sheet on a lightly floured surface. Roll the pastry sheet into a 12-inch square. Cut into **36** (2-inch) squares. Press the pastry squares into the muffin-pan cups. Brush the top edges of the pastry squares with the egg. Prick the centers of the pastries with a fork.

3. Bake for 10 minutes or until the pastries are golden brown. Using the back of a spoon, press down the centers of the hot pastries to make an indentation. Let the pastries cool in the pans on wire racks for 10 minutes. Remove the pastry cups from the pans and let cool completely on wire racks.

4. Beat the cream cheese in a medium bowl with an electric mixer on medium speed until smooth. Beat in the lemon curd. Fold in the whipped topping.

5. Pipe or spoon **about 1 teaspoon** cheese mixture into **each** pastry cup. Refrigerate for 10 minutes or until the set. Top **each** tartlet with **1** raspberry.

Haystack Snacks

Makes 24 servings

PREP TIME
15 minutes

1 package (10 ounces) peanut butter chips
1 tablespoon shortening
1 cup chow mein noodles
1 cup Pepperidge Farm® Goldfish® Colors Crackers

1. Line a baking sheet with wax paper.

2. Place the chips and shortening into a medium microwavable bowl. Microwave on MEDIUM for 30 seconds. Stir. Repeat until the mixture is melted and smooth. Add the noodles and Goldfish® crackers and toss to coat.

3. Drop the mixture by tablespoonfuls onto the baking sheet. Press **1** additional Goldfish® cracker into the top of **each**. Let stand until firm.

Kitchen Tips

You can substitute your favorite flavor chips for the peanut butter chips.

For Goldfish® Coconut Haystacks, reduce the Goldfish® crackers to ¾ cup and add ¼ cup flaked coconut.

Puff Pastry Valentine Cookies

Makes 12 servings

½ of a 17.3-ounce package Pepperidge Farm® Puff Pastry Sheets (1 sheet), thawed

3 tablespoons prepared caramel topping

3 tablespoons blanched sliced almonds *or* coconut

THAW TIME
40 minutes

PREP TIME
20 minutes

BAKE TIME
10 minutes

COOL TIME
20 minutes

1. Heat the oven to 400°F.

2. Unfold the pastry sheet on a lightly floured surface. Roll the pastry sheet into a 14×10-inch rectangle. Cut out **12** (3½-inch) hearts using a cutter. Place the cut-outs onto a baking sheet. Brush with the caramel topping and sprinkle with the almonds.

3. Bake for 10 minutes or until the cookies are golden brown. Remove the cookies from the baking sheet and let cool on a wire rack for 20 minutes.

Walnut-Orange Hearts: Substitute orange marmalade for the caramel topping and chopped walnuts for the almonds.

Ice Cream Hearts: Omit the caramel topping and almonds. Sprinkle the unbaked pastry hearts with **2 tablespoons** sugar. Bake and cool as directed. Split the pastries into **2** layers. Place a small scoop of ice cream onto **each** bottom pastry layer and top with the top pastry layer. Drizzle with melted chocolate, if desired.

Tomato Soup Spice Cake

Makes 12 servings

PREP TIME
20 minutes

BAKE TIME
40 minutes

COOL TIME
20 minutes

- **2 cups all-purpose flour**
- **1⅓ cups sugar**
- **4 teaspoons baking powder**
- **1½ teaspoons ground allspice**
- **1 teaspoon baking soda**
- **1 teaspoon ground cinnamon**
- **½ teaspoon ground cloves**
- **1 can (10¾ ounces) Campbell's® Condensed Tomato Soup**
- **½ cup vegetable shortening**
- **2 eggs**
- **¼ cup water**
- ***Cream Cheese Frosting***

1. Heat the oven to 350°F. Grease **2** (8- or 9-inch) cake pans.

2. Stir the flour, sugar, baking powder, allspice, baking soda, cinnamon and cloves in a large bowl. Add the soup, shortening, eggs and water. Beat with an electric mixer on low speed just until blended. Increase the speed to high and beat for 4 minutes. Pour the batter into the pans.

3. Bake for 40 minutes or until a toothpick inserted in the centers come out clean. Let the cakes cool in the pans on a wire rack for 20 minutes. Frost with the *Cream Cheese Frosting*.

Cream Cheese Frosting: Beat **1 package** (8 ounces) cream cheese, softened, **2 tablespoons** milk and **1 teaspoon** vanilla extract in a medium bowl with an electric mixer on medium speed until the mixture is creamy. Slowly beat in **1 package** (16 ounces) confectioners' sugar until the frosting is desired consistency.

Kitchen Tip

The cake can also be prepared in a 13×9-inch baking pan.

Chocolate Goldfish® Pretzel Clusters

Makes 24 servings

- **1 package (12 ounces) semi-sweet chocolate pieces (about 2 cups)**
- **2½ cups Pepperidge Farm® Pretzel Goldfish® Crackers**
- **1 container (4 ounces) multi-colored nonpareil**

1. Line a baking sheet with wax paper.

2. Place the chocolate into a microwavable bowl. Microwave on MEDIUM for 30 seconds. Stir. Repeat until the chocolate is melted and smooth. Add the Goldfish® crackers and stir to coat.

3. Drop the chocolate mixture by tablespoonfuls onto the baking sheet. Sprinkle the clusters with the nonpareils.

4. Refrigerate for 30 minutes or until the clusters are firm. Keep refrigerated until ready to serve.

PREP TIME
5 minutes

COOK TIME
1 minute

CHILL TIME
30 minutes

Kitchen Tip

To wrap for gift-giving, arrange the clusters in a small box lined with colored plastic wrap.

Chocolate-Cinnamon Bread Pudding

Makes 6 servings

PREP TIME
15 minutes

BAKE TIME
40 minutes

12 slices Pepperidge Farm® Cinnamon Swirl Bread, any variety, cut into cubes (about 6 cups)
½ cup semi-sweet chocolate pieces
2½ cups milk
4 eggs
½ cup packed brown sugar
1 teaspoon vanilla extract
Sweetened whipped cream (optional)

1. Heat the oven to 350°F.

2. Place the bread cubes into a lightly greased 2-quart shallow baking dish. Sprinkle the chocolate pieces over the bread cubes. Beat the milk, eggs, brown sugar and vanilla extract in a small bowl with a fork or whisk. Pour the milk mixture over the bread cubes. Stir and press the bread cubes into the milk mixture to coat.

3. Bake for 40 minutes or until a knife inserted in the center comes out clean. Serve with the whipped cream, if desired.

Kitchen Tip

This bread pudding can be served with the whipped cream as a dessert, or with a sprinkle of confectioners' sugar as a decadent brunch dish.

Berry Bordeaux Desserts

Makes 12 servings

24 Pepperidge Farm® Bordeaux® Cookies
1 cup heavy cream
¼ cup sugar
1 teaspoon vanilla extract
3 cups mixed berries*
Mint leaves (optional)

****Use a combination of sliced strawberries, raspberries, blackberries and blueberries.***

1. Place **12** cookies into a 2-quart shallow baking dish.

2. Beat the heavy cream, **2 tablespoons** sugar and vanilla extract in a medium bowl with an electric mixer on high speed until stiff peaks form.

3. Spoon the whipped cream in the baking dish. Top with the remaining cookies. Cover and refrigerate for 3 hours or until the cookies are soft.

4. Stir the berries with the remaining sugar in a medium bowl. Spoon the berry mixture over the cookie mixture. Garnish with the mint, if desired.

PREP TIME
20 minutes

CHILL TIME
3 hours

Cranberry-Walnut Crostadas

Makes 6 servings

PREP TIME
20 minutes

COOK TIME
10 minutes

COOL TIME
20 minutes

- **1 package (10 ounces) Pepperidge Farm® Puff Pastry Shells**
- **1 cup heavy cream**
- **¼ cup sugar**
- **1½ cups toasted walnut halves, chopped**
- **1 cup dried cranberries**
- **¼ teaspoon ground cinnamon**
- ***Assorted Toppings***

1. Prepare the pastry shells according to the package directions.

2. Heat the heavy cream and sugar in a 1-quart heavy saucepan over medium heat to a boil. Cook for 5 minutes or until the mixture is thickened, stirring occasionally. Remove the saucepan from the heat. Let the mixture cool to room temperature. Stir in the walnuts, cranberries and cinnamon.

3. Divide the walnut mixture among the pastry shells. Top the filled shells with one of the *Assorted Toppings,* if desired.

Assorted Toppings: Almond-flavored **or** orange-flavored liqueur-sweetened whipped cream, crumbled Roquefort **or** other bleu cheese, wedges of Cheddar cheese.

Puff Pastry Chocolatines

Makes 12 servings

½ **of a 17.3-ounce package Pepperidge Farm® Puff Pastry Sheets (1 sheet), thawed**

1 **egg, beaten**

8 **bars (1.5 ounces *each*) milk *or* dark chocolate, chopped**

Confectioners' sugar

1. Heat the oven to 375°F.

2. Unfold the pastry sheet on a lightly floured surface. Cut the pastry sheet into **12** (3×2½-inch) rectangles. With a short side facing you, brush the top third of **each** rectangle with the egg. Place **about 1 tablespoon** chocolate in the center of **each** rectangle. Starting at the short end closest to you, roll up like a jelly roll. Place the filled pastries onto a baking sheet. Brush with the egg.

3. Bake for 15 minutes or until the pastries are golden brown. Remove the pastries from the baking sheet and let cool on a wire rack for 10 minutes. Sprinkle the pastries with the confectioners' sugar.

THAW TIME
40 minutes

PREP TIME
20 minutes

BAKE TIME
15 minutes

COOL TIME
10 minutes

Kid Pleasers

Beefy Pasta Skillet

Makes 4 servings

PREP TIME
10 minutes

COOK TIME
15 minutes

- **1 pound ground beef**
- **1 medium onion, chopped (about ½ cup)**
- **1 can (10¾ ounces) Campbell's® Condensed Tomato Soup (Regular *or* Healthy Request®)**
- **¼ cup water**
- **1 tablespoon Worcestershire sauce**
- **½ cup shredded Cheddar cheese**
- **1½ cups corkscrew-shaped pasta (rotini), cooked and drained**

1. Cook the beef and onion in a 10-inch skillet over medium-high heat until the beef is well browned, stirring often to separate the meat. Pour off any fat.

2. Stir the soup, water, Worcestershire, cheese and pasta in the skillet and cook until the mixture is hot and bubbling.

Kitchen Tip

You can substitute 1 cup uncooked elbow pasta, cooked and drained, for the corkscrew pasta, if you like.

Fontina Turkey Panini

Makes 2 sandwiches

PREP TIME
5 minutes

COOK TIME
10 minutes

4 slices Pepperidge Farm® Farmhouse Sourdough Bread

Olive oil

2 tablespoons honey mustard salad dressing

4 slices fontina cheese

2 slices smoked turkey

4 bread-and-butter pickle sandwich slices

1. Brush one side of the bread slices with the oil.

2. Turn **2** bread slices oil-side down. Spread **each** with **1 tablespoon** salad dressing. Top **each** with **2** cheese slices, **1** turkey slice, **2** pickle slices and the remaining bread slices, oil-side up.

3. Heat a grill pan or skillet over medium heat. Add the sandwiches and cook for 4 minutes or until they're lightly browned on both sides and the cheese is melted.

Kitchen Tip

Try pressing down on the sandwiches with a spatula during cooking. It will help the different ingredients melt together.

Turkey Sausage & Tortellini in Creamy Tomato Basil Sauce

Makes 6 servings

- 1 pound Italian-style turkey sausage, casing removed
- 1 can (10¾ ounces) Campbell's® Condensed Cream of Chicken Soup (Regular *or* 98% Fat Free)
- ½ cup water
- 1 can (14.5 ounces) diced tomatoes, undrained
- 1 pound frozen cheese-filled tortellini
- 2 tablespoons chopped fresh basil leaves
- Grated Parmesan cheese

1. Cook the sausage in a 10-inch skillet over medium-high heat until well browned, stirring frequently to separate the meat. Pour off any fat.

2. Stir the soup, water and tomatoes into the skillet. Heat to a boil. Add the tortellini and reduce the heat to low. Cook for about 5 minutes or until the tortellini is tender but still firm.

3. Stir in the basil. Serve with the cheese, if desired.

PREP TIME
5 minutes

COOK TIME
15 minutes

Tuna & Pasta Cheddar Melt

Makes 4 servings

PREP TIME
10 minutes

COOK TIME
15 minutes

1 can (10½ ounces) Campbell's® Condensed Chicken Broth

1 soup can water

3 cups *uncooked* corkscrew-shaped pasta (rotini)

1 can (10¾ ounces) Campbell's® Condensed Cream of Mushroom Soup (Regular *or* 98% Fat Free)

1 cup milk

1 can (about 6 ounces) tuna, drained and flaked

1 cup shredded Cheddar cheese (about 4 ounces)

2 tablespoons Italian-seasoned dry bread crumbs

2 teaspoons butter, melted

1. Heat the broth and water in a 12-inch skillet over medium-high heat to a boil. Stir in the pasta. Reduce the heat to medium. Cook until the pasta is tender, stirring often. Do not drain.

2. Stir the soup, milk and tuna in the skillet. Top with the cheese. Stir the bread crumbs and butter in a small bowl. Sprinkle over the tuna mixture. Cook until the cheese is melted.

Chicken Nacho Tacos

Makes 4 servings

PREP TIME
15 minutes

COOK TIME
10 minutes

- **1 tablespoon vegetable oil**
- **1 medium onion, chopped (about ½ cup)**
- **½ teaspoon chili powder**
- **1 can (10¾ ounces) Campbell's® Condensed Fiesta Nacho Cheese Soup**
- **2 cans (4.5 ounces *each*) Swanson® Premium White Chunk Chicken Breast in Water, drained**
- **8 taco shells, warmed**
- **Shredded lettuce**
- **Chopped tomato**

1. Heat the oil in a 10-inch skillet over medium-high heat. Add the onion and chili powder and cook until the onion is tender, stirring often.

2. Stir the soup and chicken in the skillet and cook until the mixture is hot and bubbling. Spoon the chicken mixture into the taco shells. Top with the lettuce and tomato.

Cheddar Broccoli Frittata

Makes 4 servings

PREP TIME
10 minutes

COOK TIME
15 minutes

- **6 eggs**
- **1 can (10¾ ounces) Campbell's® Condensed Broccoli Cheese Soup (Regular *or* 98% Fat Free)**
- **¼ cup milk**
- **⅛ teaspoon ground black pepper**
- **1 tablespoon butter**
- **2 cups sliced mushrooms (about 6 ounces)**
- **1 large onion, chopped (about 1 cup)**
- **1 small zucchini, sliced (about 1 cup)**
- **¼ cup shredded Cheddar cheese**
- **1 green onion, chopped (about 2 tablespoons)**

1. Beat the eggs, soup, milk and black pepper in a medium bowl with a fork or whisk.

2. Heat the butter in a 12-inch ovenproof nonstick skillet over medium heat. Add the mushrooms, onion and zucchini and cook until tender. Stir in the egg mixture. Reduce the heat to low. Cook for 5 minutes or until the eggs are set but still moist.

3. Heat the broiler. Sprinkle the cheese over the egg mixture. Broil the frittata with the top 4 inches from the heat for 2 minutes or until the top is golden brown. Sprinkle with the green onion.

Simply Quick Macaroni & Cheese

Makes 6 servings

- **1¾ cups Swanson® Chicken Broth (Regular, Natural Goodness® *or* Certified Organic)**
- **¼ cup all-purpose flour**
- **⅛ teaspoon ground black pepper**
- **½ cup skim milk**
- **5 slices process American cheese, cut up**
- **3 cups elbow pasta, cooked and drained**

PREP TIME
20 minutes

COOK TIME
10 minutes

1. Stir the broth, flour, black pepper and milk in a 4-quart saucepan until the mixture is smooth. Cook and stir over medium heat until the mixture boils and thickens.

2. Stir the cheese in the saucepan. Cook and stir until cheese is melted. Add the pasta and toss to coat.

Simple Creamy Chicken Risotto

Makes 4 servings

PREP TIME
10 minutes

COOK TIME
35 minutes

- **1 tablespoon vegetable oil**
- **4 skinless, boneless chicken breast halves (about 1 pound), cut into 1-inch pieces**
- **1 can (10¾ ounces) Campbell's® Condensed Cream of Mushroom with Roasted Garlic Soup**
- **1 can (10½ ounces) Campbell's® Condensed Chicken Broth**
- **¾ cup water**
- **1 small carrot, shredded (about ¼ cup)**
- **2 green onions, sliced (about ¼ cup)**
- **1 tablespoon grated Parmesan cheese**
- **1 cup *uncooked* regular long-grain white rice**

1. Heat the oil in a 10-inch skillet over medium-high heat. Add the chicken and cook until well browned, stirring often.

2. Stir the soup, broth, water, carrot, green onions and cheese in the skillet and heat to a boil. Stir in the rice. Reduce the heat to low. Cover and cook for 25 minutes or until the chicken is cooked through and the rice is tender.

Quick Creamy Chicken & Corn

Makes 4 servings

- 1 tablespoon vegetable oil
- 4 skinless, boneless chicken breast halves (about 1 pound)
- 1 can (10¾ ounces) Campbell's® Condensed Cream of Chicken Soup (Regular *or* 98% Fat Free)
- ¾ cup water
- ½ teaspoon poultry seasoning
- 1 package (10 ounces) frozen whole kernel corn
- 2 cups refrigerated cubed potatoes
- 2 tablespoons chopped fresh parsley
- 1 cup shredded Cheddar cheese (about 4 ounces)

1. Heat the oil in a 10-inch skillet over medium-high heat. Add the chicken and cook for 10 minutes or until well browned on both sides.

2. Stir the soup, water, poultry seasoning, corn and potatoes into the skillet. Heat to a boil. Reduce the heat to low. Cover and cook for 10 minutes or until the chicken is cooked through. Stir in the parsley and sprinkle with the cheese.

PREP TIME
15 minutes

COOK TIME
25 minutes

Skillet Mac & Beef

Makes 4 servings

PREP TIME
5 minutes

COOK TIME
15 minutes

- 1 **pound ground beef**
- 1 **medium onion, chopped (about ½ cup)**
- 1 **can (10¾ ounces) Campbell's® Condensed Cream of Celery Soup (Regular *or* 98% Fat Free)**
- ¼ **cup ketchup**
- 1 **tablespoon Worcestershire sauce**
- 1½ **cups corkscrew-shaped pasta (rotini), cooked and drained**

1. Cook the beef and onion in a 10-inch skillet over medium-high heat until the beef is well browned, stirring frequently to separate the meat. Pour off any fat.

2. Stir the soup, ketchup, Worcestershire and pasta into the skillet. Reduce the heat to medium. Cook until the mixture is hot and bubbling, stirring frequently.

contents

205

257

270

Poultry Creations

Creamy Blush Sauce with Turkey and Penne

Makes 8 servings

PREP TIME
10 minutes

COOK TIME
7 hours

STAND TIME
10 minutes

Kitchen Tip

Substitute 8 bone-in chicken thighs (about 2 pounds) for the turkey thighs. Serves 4.

4 turkey thighs, skin removed (about 3 pounds)
1 jar (1 pound 9.75 ounces) Prego® Chunky Garden Mushroom & Green Pepper Italian Sauce
½ teaspoon crushed red pepper
½ cup half-and-half
Hot cooked penne pasta
Grated Parmesan cheese

1. Place the turkey into a 3½- to 5-quart slow cooker. Pour the Italian sauce over the turkey and sprinkle with the red pepper.

2. Cover and cook on LOW for 7 to 8 hours* or until the turkey is cooked through. Remove the turkey from the cooker to a cutting board. Let stand for 10 minutes. Remove the turkey meat from the bones.

3. Stir the turkey meat and the half-and-half into the cooker. Spoon the turkey mixture over the pasta. Sprinkle with the cheese.

**Or on HIGH for 4 to 5 hours.*

Savory Slow-Cooked Chicken Cacciatore

Makes 6 servings

PREP TIME
20 minutes

COOK TIME
7 hours 20 minutes

- **1 tablespoon olive oil**
- **3 pounds chicken parts, skin removed**
- **4 cloves garlic, minced**
- **2 teaspoons Italian seasoning, crushed**
- **1 can (28 ounces) crushed tomatoes in purée**
- **1 pound mushrooms, cut in half (about 5 cups)**
- **2 medium onions, chopped (about 2 cups)**
- **1 medium green pepper, cut into 2-inch-long strips (about 1½ cups)**
- **1½ cups Swanson® Chicken Stock**
- **¼ cup cornstarch**
- **1 package (16 ounces) pappardelle *or* fettuccine, cooked and drained**

Kitchen Tip

This recipe is delicious sprinkled with shredded Parmesan cheese before serving.

1. Heat the oil in a 12-inch skillet over medium-high heat. Add the chicken and cook until well browned on all sides.

2. Stir the garlic, Italian seasoning, tomatoes, mushrooms, onions, green pepper and **1 cup** stock in a 6-quart slow cooker. Add the chicken and turn to coat.

3. Cover and cook on LOW 7 to 8 hours* or until the chicken is cooked through. Remove the chicken from the cooker and keep warm.

4. Stir the cornstarch and remaining stock in a small bowl until the mixture is smooth. Stir the cornstarch mixture in the cooker. Cover and cook on HIGH for 10 minutes or until the mixture boils and thickens. Serve with the chicken and pappardelle.

**Or on HIGH for 4 to 5 hours.*

Golden Chicken with Noodles

Makes 8 servings

PREP TIME
5 minutes

COOK TIME
7 hours

- **2 cans (10¾ ounces *each*) Campbell's® Condensed Cream of Chicken Soup (Regular *or* 98% Fat Free)**
- **½ cup water**
- **¼ cup lemon juice**
- **1 tablespoon Dijon-style mustard**
- **1½ teaspoons garlic powder**
- **8 large carrots, thickly sliced (about 6 cups)**
- **8 skinless, boneless chicken breast halves (about 2 pounds)**
- **4 cups egg noodles, cooked and drained**
- **Chopped fresh parsley**

1. Stir the soup, water, lemon juice, mustard, garlic powder and carrots in a 3½-quart slow cooker. Add the chicken and turn to coat.

2. Cover and cook on LOW for 7 to 8 hours* or until the chicken is cooked through. Serve with the noodles. Sprinkle with the parsley.

**Or on HIGH for 4 to 5 hours.*

Turkey Fajita Wraps

Makes 8 servings

PREP TIME
10 minutes

COOK TIME
6 hours

- **2 cups Pace® Picante Sauce**
- **2 large green *or* red peppers, cut into 2-inch-long strips (about 4 cups)**
- **1½ cups frozen whole kernel corn, thawed**
- **1 tablespoon chili powder**
- **2 tablespoons lime juice**
- **3 cloves garlic, minced**
- **2 pounds turkey breast cutlets, cut into 4-inch-long strips**
- **16 flour tortillas (8-inch), warmed**
- **Shredded Mexican cheese blend**

1. Stir the picante sauce, peppers, corn, chili powder, lime juice, garlic and turkey in a 4-quart slow cooker.

2. Cover and cook on LOW for 6 to 7 hours* or until the turkey is cooked through.

3. Spoon **about ½ cup** of the turkey mixture down the center of **each** tortilla. Top with the cheese. Fold the tortillas around the filling.

**Or on HIGH for 3 to 4 hours.*

Kitchen Tip

Delicious served with an assortment of additional toppers: sliced green onions, sliced ripe olives, shredded lettuce, sliced jalapeño peppers, sour cream and/or chopped fresh cilantro.

Pacific Island Chicken & Rice

Makes 8 servings

- 2 cans (10½ ounces ***each***) Campbell's® Condensed Chicken Broth
- 1 cup water
- ¼ cup soy sauce
- 2 cloves garlic, minced
- 8 skinless, boneless chicken thighs (about 2 pounds), cut into 1½-inch pieces
- 1 medium green ***or*** red pepper, cut into 1½-inch pieces (about 1 cup)
- 4 green onions, cut into 2-inch pieces (about 1 cup)
- 1 can (20 ounces) pineapple chunks in juice, undrained
- 1 cup ***uncooked*** regular long-grain white rice
- Toasted sliced almonds

1. Stir the broth, water, soy sauce, garlic, chicken, pepper, onions, pineapple with juice and rice in 6-quart slow cooker.

2. Cover and cook on LOW for 7 to 8 hours* or until chicken is cooked through.

3. Sprinkle with the almonds before serving.

**Or on HIGH for 4 to 5 hours.*

PREP TIME
20 minutes

COOK TIME
7 hours

Kitchen Tip

To toast almonds, arrange almonds in single layer in a shallow baking pan. Bake at 350°F. for 10 minutes or until lightly browned.

Chicken in Creamy Sun-Dried Tomato Sauce

Makes 8 servings

PREP TIME
15 minutes

COOK TIME
7 hours

- **2 cans (10¾ ounces *each*) Campbell's® Condensed Cream of Chicken with Herbs Soup *or* Campbell's® Condensed Cream of Chicken Soup**
- **1 cup Chablis *or* other dry white wine***
- **¼ cup coarsely chopped pitted kalamata *or* oil-cured olives**
- **2 tablespoons drained capers**
- **2 cloves garlic, minced**
- **1 can (14 ounces) artichoke hearts, drained and chopped**
- **1 cup drained and coarsely chopped sun-dried tomatoes**
- **8 skinless, boneless chicken breast halves (about 2 pounds)**
- **½ cup chopped fresh basil leaves (optional)**
- **Hot cooked rice, egg noodles *or* mashed potatoes**

****You can substitute Swanson® Chicken Broth for the wine, if desired.***

1. Stir the soup, wine, olives, capers, garlic, artichokes and tomatoes in a 3½-quart slow cooker. Add the chicken and turn to coat.

2. Cover and cook on LOW for 7 to 8 hours** or until the chicken is cooked through. Sprinkle with the basil, if desired. Serve with the rice.

***Or on HIGH for 4 to 5 hours.*

Mahogany Wings

Makes 18 wings

PREP TIME
6 hours 30 minutes

COOK TIME
4 hours

- **6 pounds chicken wings (about 36 wings)**
- **1 can (10½ ounces) Campbell's® Condensed Beef Broth**
- **2 bunches green onions, chopped**
- **1 cup soy sauce**
- **1 cup plum sauce**
- **6 cloves garlic, minced**
- **½ cup light molasses *or* honey**
- **¼ cup cider vinegar**
- **1 tablespoon cornstarch**

1. Cut off the chicken wing ends and discard. Cut the chicken wings in half at the joint.

2. Stir the broth, onions, soy sauce, plum sauce, garlic, molasses and vinegar in a large nonmetallic bowl. Add the chicken and stir to coat. Cover and refrigerate for 6 hours or overnight.

3. Stir ½ **cup** of the marinade and the cornstarch in a small bowl. Add the cornstarch and chicken mixture to the cooker.

4. Cover and cook on HIGH for 4 to 5 hours* or until the chicken is cooked through.

**Or on LOW for 7 to 8 hours.*

West African Chicken Stew

Makes 6 servings

PREP TIME
15 minutes

COOK TIME
7 hours

- ½ cup all-purpose flour
- 2 teaspoons pumpkin pie spice
- 1 teaspoon paprika
- ½ teaspoon cracked black pepper
- 6 bone-in chicken thighs
- 6 chicken drumsticks
- 2 tablespoons vegetable oil
- 1 can (10¾ ounces) Campbell's® Condensed French Onion Soup
- ½ cup water
- 1 cup raisins*
- ½ cup orange juice
- 1 teaspoon grated orange peel
- 2 tablespoons chopped fresh parsley ***or*** cilantro leaves
- 6 cups hot cooked couscous

***You may substitute chopped prunes *or* apricots for the raisins, if you like.**

1. Mix the flour, pumpkin pie spice, paprika and black pepper on a plate. Coat the chicken with the flour mixture.

2. Heat the oil in a 12-inch skillet over medium heat. Add the chicken and cook for 10 minutes or until well browned.

3. Stir the soup, water, raisins, orange juice and orange peel in a 6-quart slow cooker. Add the chicken and turn to coat.

4. Cover and cook on LOW for 7 to 8 hours** or until the chicken is cooked through.

5. Stir the parsley into the cooker. Serve with the couscous.

***Or on HIGH for 4 to 5 hours.*

Slow Cooker Orange Chicken

Makes 4 servings

PREP TIME
10 minutes

COOK TIME
8 hours

- **1½ cups Swanson® Chicken Stock**
- **¼ cup teriyaki sauce**
- **3 cloves garlic, minced**
- **¾ cup orange marmalade**
- **4 green onions, sliced (about ½ cup)**
- **2 tablespoons cornstarch**
- **8 chicken thighs, skin removed (about 2 pounds)**
- **½ cup walnut pieces**
- **Hot cooked rice**

1. Stir the stock, teriyaki sauce, garlic, marmalade, **¼ cup** green onions and cornstarch in a 6-quart slow cooker. Add the chicken and turn to coat.

2. Cover and cook on LOW for 8 to 9 hours* or until the chicken is cooked through. Sprinkle with the walnuts and remaining green onions. Serve with the rice.

**Or on HIGH for 4 to 5 hours.*

Herbed Turkey Breast

Makes 8 servings

PREP TIME
10 minutes

COOK TIME
8 hours

STAND TIME
10 minutes

Kitchen Tip

If using a frozen turkey breast, thaw it before cooking.

- **1 can (10¾ ounces) Campbell's® Condensed Cream of Mushroom Soup (Regular *or* 98% Fat Free)**
- **½ cup water**
- **4½- to 5-pound turkey breast**
- **1 teaspoon poultry seasoning**
- **1 tablespoon chopped fresh parsley**
- **Hot mashed potatoes**

1. Stir the soup and water in a 3½- to 6-quart slow cooker. Rinse the turkey with cold water and pat it dry. Rub the turkey with the poultry seasoning and place it into the cooker. Sprinkle with the parsley.

2. Cover and cook on LOW for 8 to 9 hours* or until the turkey is cooked through. Let the turkey stand for 10 minutes before slicing. Serve with the soup mixture and mashed potatoes.

**Or on HIGH for 4 to 5 hours.*

Curried Turkey Cutlets

Makes 8 servings

- **2 cans (10¾ ounces *each*) Campbell's® Condensed Cream of Chicken Soup (Regular *or* 98% Fat Free)**
- **2 tablespoons water**
- **1 tablespoon curry powder**
- **½ teaspoon cracked black pepper**
- **8 turkey breast cutlets (about 2 pounds)**
- **¼ cup heavy cream**
- **½ cup seedless red grapes, cut in half**
- **Hot cooked rice *or* seasoned rice blend**

PREP TIME
10 minutes

COOK TIME
6 hours

1. Stir the soup, water, curry powder and black pepper in a 3½- to 4-quart slow cooker. Add the turkey and turn to coat.

2. Cover and cook on LOW for 6 to 7 hours* or until the turkey is cooked through.

3. Stir the cream and grapes into the cooker. Serve with the rice.

**Or on HIGH for 3 to 4 hours.*

Kitchen Tip

This recipe is delicious served with any of these toppers: chutney, toasted coconut, sliced almonds and/or raisins.

Slow Cooker Chicken & Dumplings

Makes 8 servings

PREP TIME
20 minutes

COOK TIME
7 hours 30 minutes

- **6 skinless, boneless chicken breast halves (about 1½ pounds), cut into 1-inch pieces**
- **2 medium Yukon Gold potatoes, cut into 1-inch pieces (about 2 cups)**
- **2 cups whole baby carrots**
- **2 stalks celery, sliced (about 1 cup)**
- **2 cans (10¾ ounces *each*) Campbell's® Condensed Cream of Chicken Soup (Regular *or* 98% Fat Free)**
- **1 cup water**
- **1 teaspoon dried thyme leaves, crushed**
- **¼ teaspoon ground black pepper**
- **2 cups all-purpose baking mix**
- **⅔ cup milk**

1. Place the chicken, potatoes, carrots and celery into a 6-quart slow cooker.

2. Stir the soup, water, thyme and black pepper in a small bowl. Pour the soup mixture over the chicken and vegetables.

3. Cover and cook on LOW for 7 to 8 hours* or until the chicken is cooked through.

4. Stir the baking mix and milk in a medium bowl. Drop the batter by spoonfuls onto the chicken mixture. Increase the heat to HIGH. Tilt the lid to vent and cook for 30 minutes or until the dumplings are cooked in the center.

**Or on HIGH for 4 to 5 hours.*

Slow Cooker Coq au Vin

Makes 6 servings

1 package (10 ounces) sliced mushrooms (about 3¾ cups)

1 bag (16 ounces) frozen whole small white onions

1 sprig fresh rosemary leaves

2 pounds skinless, boneless chicken breast halves *and/or* thighs, cut into 1-inch strips

¼ cup cornstarch

1 can (10¾ ounces) Campbell's® Condensed Golden Mushroom Soup

1 cup Burgundy *or* other dry red wine

Hot mashed *or* oven-roasted potatoes

1. Place the mushrooms, onions, rosemary and chicken into a 3½-quart slow cooker.

2. Stir the cornstarch, soup and wine in a small bowl. Pour over the chicken and vegetables.

3. Cover and cook on LOW for 8 to 9 hours*. Remove and discard the rosemary. Serve the chicken mixture with the mashed potatoes.

**Or on HIGH for 4 to 5 hours.*

PREP TIME
10 minutes

COOK TIME
8 hours

Hearty & Flavorful Meats

Beef Bourguignonne

Makes 6 servings

PREP TIME
10 minutes

COOK TIME
8 hours

- **1 can ($10\frac{3}{4}$ ounces) Campbell's® Condensed Golden Mushroom Soup**
- **1 cup Burgundy *or* other dry red wine**
- **2 cloves garlic, minced**
- **1 teaspoon dried thyme leaves, crushed**
- **2 cups small button mushrooms (about 6 ounces)**
- **2 cups fresh *or* thawed frozen baby carrots**
- **1 cup frozen small whole onions, thawed**
- **$1\frac{1}{2}$ pounds beef top round steak, $1\frac{1}{2}$-inches thick, cut into 1-inch pieces**

1. Stir the soup, wine, garlic, thyme, mushrooms, carrots, onions and beef in $3\frac{1}{2}$-quart slow cooker.

2. Cover and cook on LOW for 8 to 9 hours* or until the beef is fork-tender.

**Or on HIGH for 4 to 5 hours.*

Slow Cooker Beef & Mushroom Stew

Makes 6 servings

PREP TIME
20 minutes

COOK TIME
10 hours 15 minutes

- **1 boneless beef bottom round roast *or* chuck pot roast (about 1½ pounds), cut into 1-inch pieces**
- **Ground black pepper**
- **¼ cup all-purpose flour**
- **2 tablespoons vegetable oil**
- **1 can (10½ ounces) Campbell's® Condensed French Onion Soup**
- **1 cup Burgundy *or* other dry red wine**
- **2 cloves garlic, minced**
- **1 teaspoon Italian seasoning, crushed**
- **10 ounces mushrooms, cut in half (about 3 cups)**
- **3 medium carrots, cut into 2-inch pieces (about 1½ cups)**
- **1 cup frozen whole small white onions**
- **¼ cup water**

1. Season the beef with the black pepper. Coat the beef with **2 tablespoons** flour. Heat the oil in a 12-inch skillet over medium-high heat. Add the beef and cook until well browned, stirring often.

2. Stir the beef, soup, wine, garlic, Italian seasoning, mushrooms, carrots and onions in a 3½-quart slow cooker.

3. Cover and cook on LOW for 10 to 11 hours* or until the beef is fork-tender.

4. Stir the remaining flour and water in a small bowl until the mixture is smooth. Stir the flour mixture in the cooker. Increase the heat to HIGH. Cover and cook for 15 minutes or until the mixture boils and thickens.

**Or on HIGH for 5 to 6 hours.*

Apricot Glazed Pork Roast

Makes 8 servings

PREP TIME
5 minutes

COOK TIME
8 hours

1 can (10½ ounces) Campbell's® Condensed Chicken Broth
1 jar (18 ounces) apricot preserves
1 large onion, chopped (about 1 cup)
2 tablespoons Dijon-style mustard
1 boneless pork loin roast (about 4 pounds)

1. Stir the broth, preserves, onion and mustard in a 3½-quart slow cooker. Add the pork to the cooker, cutting to fit, if needed, and turn to coat.

2. Cover and cook on LOW for 8 to 9 hours* or until the pork is fork-tender.

Or on HIGH for 4 to 5 hours.

Kitchen Tip

For thicker sauce, mix 2 tablespoons cornstarch and 2 tablespoons water in a small bowl until smooth. Remove the pork from the cooker. Stir the cornstarch mixture in the cooker. Cover and cook on HIGH for 10 minutes or until the mixture boils and thickens.

Slow-Cooked Pulled Pork Sliders

Makes 12 mini sandwiches

PREP TIME
10 minutes

COOK TIME
8 hours

STAND TIME
10 minutes

- **1 can (10¾ ounces) Campbell's® Condensed Tomato Soup**
- **½ cup packed brown sugar**
- **¼ cup cider vinegar**
- **1 teaspoon garlic powder**
- **1 boneless pork shoulder roast (3½ to 4½ pounds)**
- **2 packages (15 ounces *each*) Pepperidge Farm® Slider Mini Sandwich Rolls**
- **Hot pepper sauce (optional)**

1. Stir the soup, brown sugar, vinegar and garlic powder in a 6-quart slow cooker. Add the pork and turn to coat.

2. Cover and cook on LOW for 8 to 9 hours* or until the pork is fork-tender. Spoon off any fat.

3. Remove the pork from the cooker to a cutting board and let stand for 10 minutes. Using 2 forks, shred the pork. Return the pork to the cooker.

4. Divide the pork mixture among the rolls. Serve with the hot pepper sauce, if desired.

**Or on HIGH for 4 to 5 hours.*

Slow Cooker Hearty Beef Stew

Makes 6 servings

PREP TIME
20 minutes

COOK TIME
10 hours 15 minutes

- **1½ pounds beef for stew, cut into 1-inch pieces**
- **Ground black pepper**
- **¼ cup all-purpose flour**
- **1 tablespoon vegetable oil**
- **1 pound medium potatoes, cut into cubes (about 3 cups)**
- **4 medium carrots, sliced (about 2 cups)**
- **2 medium onions, cut into wedges**
- **4 cloves garlic, minced**
- **3¼ cups Swanson® Beef Stock**
- **1 tablespoon Worcestershire sauce**
- **1 teaspoon dried thyme leaves, crushed**
- **1 bay leaf**
- **1 cup thawed frozen peas**

1. Season the beef with the black pepper. Coat the beef with **2 tablespoons** of the flour. Heat the oil in a 10-inch skillet over medium-high heat. Add the beef in 2 batches and cook until well browned, stirring often.

2. Place the potatoes, carrots, onions and garlic into a 5-quart slow cooker. Top with the beef. Add **3 cups** of the stock, Worcestershire, thyme and bay leaf.

3. Cover and cook on LOW for 10 to 11 hours* or until the beef is fork-tender. Remove and discard the bay leaf.

4. Stir the remaining flour and stock in a small bowl until the mixture is smooth. Stir the flour mixture and peas in the cooker. Increase the heat to HIGH. Cover and cook for 15 minutes or until the mixture boils and thickens.

**Or on HIGH for 5 to 6 hours.*

Braised Short Ribs with Red Wine Tomato Sauce

Makes 8 servings

- 4 pounds beef short ribs, cut into serving-sized pieces
- 2⅔ cups Prego® Fresh Mushroom Italian Sauce
- 1 cup dry red wine
- 1 bag fresh *or* frozen whole baby carrots
- 1 large onion, chopped (about 1 cup)
- Hot cooked rice

PREP TIME
10 minutes

COOK TIME
7 hours

1. Season the ribs as desired.

2. Stir the Italian sauce, wine, carrots and onion in a 3½-quart slow cooker. Add the ribs and turn to coat.

3. Cover and cook on LOW for 7 to 8 hours* or until the ribs are fork-tender. Serve with the rice.

**Or on HIGH for 4 to 5 hours.*

Picadillo

Makes 8 servings

PREP TIME
15 minutes

COOK TIME
7 hours

- **1½ pounds ground beef**
- **2 large onions, diced (about 2 cups)**
- **1¾ cups Swanson® Beef Stock**
- **1 jar (8 ounces) Pace® Picante Sauce**
- **1 tablespoon tomato paste**
- **1 tablespoon chili powder**
- **1 teaspoon ground cumin**
- **½ cup raisins**
- **½ cup toasted slivered almonds**
- **Hot cooked rice**

1. Cook the beef and onions in a 12-inch skillet over medium-high heat until the beef is well browned, stirring often to separate the meat. Pour off any fat.

2. Stir the beef mixture, stock, picante sauce, tomato paste, chili powder, cumin and raisins in a 6-quart slow cooker.

3. Cover and cook on LOW for 7 to 8 hours*. Top the beef mixture with the almonds. Serve with the rice.

**Or on HIGH for 4 to 5 hours.*

Asian Tomato Beef

Makes 8 servings

PREP TIME
10 minutes

COOK TIME
7 hours 15 minutes

- **2 cans (10¾ ounces *each*) Campbell's® Condensed Tomato Soup**
- **⅓ cup soy sauce**
- **⅓ cup vinegar**
- **1½ teaspoons garlic powder**
- **¼ teaspoon ground black pepper**
- **1 boneless beef round steak (3 to 3½ pounds), cut into strips**
- **6 cups broccoli florets**
- **Hot cooked rice**

1. Stir the soup, soy sauce, vinegar, garlic powder, black pepper and beef in a 3½-quart slow cooker.

2. Cover and cook on LOW for 7 to 8 hours* or until the beef is fork-tender.

3. Stir in the broccoli. Increase the heat to HIGH. Cover and cook for 15 minutes or until the broccoli is tender-crisp. Serve the beef mixture with the rice.

**Or on HIGH for 4 to 5 hours.*

Slow-Simmered Pot Roast with Garden Vegetables

Makes 6 servings

PREP TIME
15 minutes

COOK TIME
10 hours

4 **medium potatoes, cut into quarters (about 4 cups)**
2 **cups fresh *or* frozen whole baby carrots**
2 **stalks celery, cut into 1-inch pieces (about 1½ cups)**
1 **beef bottom round roast, trimmed of all fat (about 2 pounds)**
½ **teaspoon ground black pepper**
1 **carton (18.3 ounces) Campbell's® V8® Butternut Squash Soup**
1 **tablespoon minced garlic**
Fresh parsley

1. Place the potatoes, carrots and celery into a 4- to 6-quart slow cooker. Season the beef with the black pepper and place on the vegetables.

2. Add the soup and garlic and toss to coat.

3. Cover and cook on LOW for 10 to 11 hours or until the beef is fork-tender. Garnish with parsley, if desired.

Kitchen Tip

For thicker gravy, stir ¼ cup all-purpose flour and ½ cup water in a small bowl until it's smooth. Remove the beef from the slow cooker. Stir in the flour mixture. Cover and cook on HIGH for 10 minutes or until the mixture boils and thickens.

Chipotle Chili

Makes 8 servings

PREP TIME
15 minutes

COOK TIME
8 hours

- **1 jar (16 ounces) Pace® Picante Sauce**
- **1 cup water**
- **2 tablespoons chili powder**
- **1 teaspoon ground chipotle chile pepper**
- **1 large onion, chopped (about 1 cup)**
- **2 pounds beef for stew, cut into ½-inch pieces**
- **1 can (about 19 ounces) red kidney beans, rinsed and drained**
- **Shredded Cheddar cheese (optional)**
- **Sour cream (optional)**

1. Stir the picante sauce, water, chili powder, chipotle chile pepper, onion, beef and beans in a 3½-quart slow cooker.

2. Cover and cook on LOW for 8 to 9 hours* or until the beef is fork-tender. Serve with the cheese and sour cream, if desired.

**Or on HIGH for 4 to 5 hours.*

Weekday Pot Roast & Vegetables

Makes 8 servings

PREP TIME
15 minutes

COOK TIME
10 hours

1 boneless beef bottom round roast *or* chuck pot roast (2 to 2½ pounds)
1 teaspoon garlic powder
1 tablespoon vegetable oil
1 pound potatoes, cut into wedges
3 cups fresh *or* frozen whole baby carrots
1 medium onion, thickly sliced (about ¾ cup)
2 teaspoons dried basil leaves, crushed
2 cans (10¼ ounces *each*) Campbell's® Beef Gravy

1. Season the beef with the garlic powder. Heat the oil in a 10-inch skillet over medium-high heat. Add the beef and cook until well browned on all sides.

2. Place the potatoes, carrots and onion in a 3½-quart slow cooker. Sprinkle with the basil. Add the beef to the cooker. Pour the gravy over the beef and vegetables.

3. Cover and cook on LOW for 10 to 11 hours* or until the beef is fork-tender.

**Or on HIGH for 5 to 6 hours.*

Golden Mushroom Pork & Apples

Makes 8 servings

2 cans (10¾ ounces *each*) Campbell's® Condensed Golden Mushroom Soup
½ cup water
1 tablespoon packed brown sugar
1 tablespoon Worcestershire sauce
1 teaspoon dried thyme leaves, crushed
8 boneless pork chops, ¾-inch thick (about 2 pounds)
4 large Granny Smith apples, sliced
2 large onions, sliced (about 2 cups)

PREP TIME
10 minutes

COOK TIME
8 hours

1. Stir the soup, water, brown sugar, Worcestershire and thyme in a 3½-quart slow cooker. Add the pork, apples and onions.

2. Cover and cook on LOW for 8 to 9 hours* or until the pork is cooked through.

**Or on HIGH for 4 to 5 hours.*

Swiss-Style Veal and Mushrooms

Makes 4 servings

PREP TIME
10 minutes

COOK TIME
7 hours 5 minutes

1¾ cups Swanson® Chicken Stock
1 can (10¾ ounces) Campbell's® Condensed Cream of Potato Soup
1 teaspoon dried thyme leaves, crushed
1½ pounds veal for stew
1 package (8 ounces) sliced mushrooms
8 green onions, sliced (about 1 cup)
2 tablespoons all-purpose flour
¼ cup water
1 cup shredded Swiss cheese (about 4 ounces)
Hot cooked egg noodles
Freshly ground black pepper

1. Stir the stock, soup, thyme, veal, mushrooms and green onions in a 3½-quart slow cooker. Cover and cook on LOW for 7 to 8 hours or until the veal is fork-tender.

2. Stir the flour and water in a small bowl until the mixture is smooth. Stir the flour mixture in the cooker. Turn the heat to HIGH. Cover and cook for 5 minutes or until the mixture boils and thickens.

3. Stir in the cheese. Serve over the noodles. Season with the black pepper.

Kitchen Tip

Veal for stew is a good way to enjoy veal for less. It's much less expensive than chops or tenderloin cuts and tastes wonderful in this recipe.

Melt-in-Your-Mouth Short Ribs

Makes 6 servings

PREP TIME
10 minutes

COOK TIME
8 hours

- **6 serving-sized pieces beef short ribs (about 3 pounds)**
- **2 tablespoons packed brown sugar**
- **3 cloves garlic, minced**
- **1 teaspoon dried thyme leaves, crushed**
- **¼ cup all-purpose flour**
- **1 can (10½ ounces) Campbell's® Condensed French Onion Soup**
- **1 bottle (12 fluid ounces) dark ale *or* beer**
- **Hot mashed potatoes *or* egg noodles**

1. Place the beef into a 5-quart slow cooker. Add the brown sugar, garlic, thyme and flour and toss to coat.

2. Stir the soup and ale in a small bowl. Pour over the beef.

3. Cover and cook on LOW for 8 to 9 hours* or until the beef is fork-tender. Serve with the mashed potatoes.

**Or on HIGH for 4 to 5 hours.*

Slow Cooker Mole-Style Pulled Pork

Makes 12 servings

PREP TIME
10 minutes

COOK TIME
8 hours

1 can (10½ ounces) Campbell's® Condensed French Onion Soup
¼ cup water
1 tablespoon chili powder
1 tablespoon brown sugar
1 teaspoon ground cumin
1 teaspoon ground cinnamon
1 boneless pork shoulder roast (3½ to 4½ pounds)
2 tablespoons semi-sweet chocolate pieces
12 flour tortillas (8-inch), warmed
6 plum tomatoes, seeded and chopped
¼ cup chopped fresh cilantro leaves

1. Stir the soup, water, chili powder, brown sugar, cumin and cinnamon in a 6-quart slow cooker. Add the pork and turn to coat.

2. Cover and cook on LOW for 8 to 9 hours* or until the pork is fork-tender. Remove the pork to a cutting board. Using 2 forks, shred the pork. Add the chocolate to the cooker and stir until melted. Return the pork to the cooker.

3. Place **about ½ cup** pork mixture onto **half** of **each** tortilla. Top with the tomatoes and cilantro. Fold the tortillas over the filling.

**Or on HIGH for 5 to 6 hours.*

Spaghetti Bolognese

Makes 8 servings

6 slices bacon, cut into ½-inch pieces
1 large onion, diced (about 1 cup)
3 cloves garlic, minced
2 pounds ground beef
4 cups Prego® Traditional Italian Sauce
1 cup milk
1 pound spaghetti, cooked and drained*
Grated Parmesan cheese

Reserve some of the cooking water from the spaghetti. You can use it to adjust the consistency of the finished sauce, if you like.

PREP TIME
15 minutes

COOK TIME
4 hours

1. Cook the bacon in a 12-inch skillet over medium-high heat until crisp. Remove the bacon from the skillet. Pour off all but **1 tablespoon** of the drippings.

2. Add the onion and cook in the hot drippings until tender. Add the garlic and beef and cook until the beef is well browned, stirring often. Pour off any fat.

3. Stir the bacon, beef mixture, Italian sauce and milk in a 6-quart slow cooker.

4. Cover and cook on HIGH for 4 to 5 hours.** Toss the spaghetti with the sauce. Sprinkle with the cheese, as desired.

***Or on LOW for 7 to 8 hours.*

Veal Stew with Garden Vegetables

Makes 6 servings

PREP TIME
25 minutes

COOK TIME
8 hours

- **2 to 2½ pounds veal for stew, cut into 1-inch pieces**
- **Ground black pepper**
- **2 tablespoons olive oil**
- **1 bag (16 ounces) fresh *or* thawed frozen whole baby carrots**
- **1 large onion, diced (about 1 cup)**
- **5 cloves garlic, minced**
- **¼ cup all-purpose flour**
- **2 cups Swanson® Chicken Stock**
- **½ teaspoon dried rosemary leaves, crushed**
- **1 can (14.5 ounces) diced tomatoes**
- **1 cup frozen peas, thawed**
- **Hot cooked rice *or* barley**

1. Season the veal with the black pepper.

2. Heat the oil in a 12-inch skillet over medium-high heat. Add the veal in 2 batches and cook until well browned, stirring often.

3. Place the veal, carrots, onion and garlic into a 4-quart slow cooker. Sprinkle with the flour and toss to coat.

4. Stir in the stock, rosemary and tomatoes. Cover and cook on LOW for 7 to 8 hours*.

5. Add the peas to the cooker. Cover and cook for 1 hour or until the veal is fork-tender. Season with additional black pepper. Serve the veal mixture with the rice.

**Kitchen Tips*

You can substitute skinless, boneless chicken thighs for the veal.

For more flavorful rice or barley, cook it in Swanson® Chicken Broth.

**Or on HIGH for 4 to 5 hours.*

Slow-Cooked Carolina Beef Brisket

Makes 8 servings

PREP TIME
10 minutes

COOK TIME
8 hours

- **1 jar (16 ounces) Pace® Picante Sauce**
- **½ cup molasses**
- **¼ cup cider vinegar**
- **2 tablespoons reduced-sodium Worcestershire sauce**
- **1 large onion, sliced (about 1 cup)**
- **1 beef brisket (3 to 4 pounds)**

1. Stir the picante sauce, molasses, vinegar, Worcestershire and onion in a 5-quart slow cooker. Add the beef, trimming to fit, if needed, and turn to coat.

2. Cover and cook on LOW for 8 to 9 hours* or until the beef is fork-tender.

**Or on HIGH for 4 to 5 hours.*

Slow Cooker Savory Pot Roast

Makes 6 servings

PREP TIME
10 minutes

COOK TIME
8 hours

- **1 can (10¾ ounces) Campbell's® Condensed Cream of Mushroom Soup (Regular *or* 98% Fat Free)**
- **1 envelope (about 1 ounce) dry onion soup and recipe mix**
- **6 small red potatoes, cut in half**
- **6 medium carrots, cut into 2-inch pieces (about 3 cups)**
- **1 boneless beef bottom round roast *or* chuck pot roast (3 to 3½ pounds)**

1. Stir the mushroom soup, soup mix, potatoes and carrots in a 4½-quart slow cooker. Add the beef and turn to coat.

2. Cover and cook on LOW for 8 to 9 hours* or until the beef is fork-tender.

**Or on HIGH for 4 to 5 hours.*

On the Side

Slow-Cooked Ratatouille with Penne

Makes 4 servings

PREP TIME
25 minutes

COOK TIME
5 hours 30 minutes

- **1 can (10¾ ounces) Campbell's® Condensed Tomato Soup**
- **1 tablespoon olive oil**
- **⅛ teaspoon ground black pepper**
- **1 small eggplant, peeled and cut into ½-inch cubes (about 5 cups)**
- **1 medium zucchini, thinly sliced (about 1½ cups)**
- **1 medium red pepper, diced (about 1 cup)**
- **1 large onion, sliced (about 1 cup)**
- **1 clove garlic, minced**
- **Hot cooked penne pasta**
- **Grated Parmesan cheese (optional)**

1. Stir the soup, oil, black pepper, eggplant, zucchini, red pepper, onion and garlic in a 4-quart slow cooker.

2. Cover and cook on LOW for 5½ to 6 hours* or until the vegetables are tender.

3. Serve the vegetable mixture over the pasta. Sprinkle with the cheese, if desired.

**Or on HIGH for 2½ to 3 hours.*

Swiss Cheese Fondue

Makes 6 servings

PREP TIME
10 minutes

COOK TIME
1 hour

Kitchen Tip

This recipe may be doubled.

1 clove garlic, cut in half
1 can (10½ ounces) Campbell's® Condensed Chicken Broth
2 cans (10¾ ounces *each*) Campbell's® Condensed Cheddar Cheese Soup
1 cup water
½ cup Chablis *or* other dry white wine
1 tablespoon Dijon-style mustard
1 tablespoon cornstarch
4 cups shredded Emmentaler *or* Gruyère cheese (about 1 pound), at room temperature
¼ teaspoon ground nutmeg
Dash ground black pepper
Pepperidge Farm® Garlic Bread, prepared and cut into cubes
Fresh vegetables

1. Rub the inside of a 5½-quart slow cooker with the cut sides of the garlic. Discard the garlic. Stir the broth, soup, water, wine, mustard, cornstarch, cheese, nutmeg and black pepper in the cooker.

2. Cover and cook on LOW for 1 hour or until the cheese is melted, stirring occasionally.

3. Serve with the bread and vegetables on skewers for dipping.

Caponata

Makes 6 servings

PREP TIME
20 minutes

COOK TIME
7 hours

4 cups eggplant, cut into 1-inch cubes
1 large onion, diced (about 1 cup)
1 can (10¾ ounces) Campbell's® Condensed Golden Mushroom Soup
1 can (about 14.5 ounces) diced tomatoes
2 stalks celery, diced (about 1 cup)
½ cup sliced green olives
2 tablespoons balsamic vinegar
1 tablespoon tomato paste
1 clove garlic, minced
½ teaspoon dried oregano leaves, crushed
¼ teaspoon crushed red pepper
Hot cooked penne pasta
Shredded Parmesan cheese

1. Stir the eggplant, onion, soup, tomatoes, celery, olives, vinegar, tomato paste, garlic, oregano and red pepper in a 6-quart slow cooker.

2. Cover and cook on LOW for 7 to 8 hours* or until the vegetables are tender. Serve over the pasta. Sprinkle with the cheese.

**Or on HIGH for 4 to 5 hours.*

Kitchen Tip

The caponata is also delicious served in pita bread, topped with crumbled feta cheese.

Southwestern Bean Medley

Makes 8 servings

PREP TIME
10 minutes

COOK TIME
7 hours

- **1¾ cups Swanson® Vegetable Broth (Regular *or* Certified Organic)**
- **1 tablespoon chili powder**
- **1 teaspoon ground cumin**
- **1 can (about 15 ounces) black beans, rinsed and drained**
- **1 can (about 15 ounces) chickpeas (garbanzo beans), rinsed and drained**
- **1 can (about 15 ounces) white kidney beans (cannellini), rinsed and drained**
- **½ cup dried lentils**
- **1 can (about 14.5 ounces) diced tomatoes and green chilies**
- **Chopped fresh cilantro leaves**

1. Stir the broth, chili powder, cumin, black beans, chickpeas, white kidney beans and lentils in a 3½-quart slow cooker.

2. Cover and cook on LOW for 6 to 7 hours*.

3. Stir in the tomatoes and green chilies. Cover and cook for 1 hour or until the beans are tender. Sprinkle with the cilantro.

**Or on HIGH for 3 to 4 hours.*

Kitchen Tip

For a complete meal, serve over hot cooked rice.

Chicken & Vegetable Bruschetta

Makes 7 servings

PREP TIME
15 minutes

COOK TIME
6 hours

STAND TIME
5 minutes

1 can (10¾ ounces) Campbell's® Condensed Cream of Mushroom Soup (Regular ***or*** 98% Fat Free)
1 can (about 14.5 ounces) diced tomatoes, drained
1 small eggplant, peeled and diced (about 2 cups)
1 large zucchini, diced (about 2 cups)
1 small onion, chopped (about ¼ cup)
1 pound skinless, boneless chicken breast halves
¼ cup shredded Parmesan cheese
2 tablespoons chopped fresh parsley ***or*** basil leaves
Thinly sliced Italian bread, toasted

1. Stir the soup, tomatoes, eggplant, zucchini and onion in a 6-quart slow cooker. Add the chicken and turn to coat.

2. Cover and cook on LOW for 6 to 7 hours* or until the chicken is fork-tender.

3. Remove the chicken from the cooker to a cutting board and let stand for 5 minutes. Using 2 forks, shred the chicken. Return the chicken to the cooker. Stir in the cheese and parsley.

4. Serve on the bread slices. Sprinkle with additional Parmesan cheese and chopped parsley, if desired.

**Or on HIGH for 4 to 5 hours.*

Kitchen Tip

The chicken mixture is also delicious over hot cooked rice or pasta.

Scalloped Potatoes

Makes 6 servings

PREP TIME
15 minutes

COOK TIME
4 hours

STAND TIME
5 minutes

Vegetable cooking spray

- **3 pounds Yukon Gold *or* Eastern potatoes, thinly sliced (about 9 cups)**
- **1 large onion, thinly sliced (about 1 cup)**
- **1 can (10¾ ounces) Campbell's® Condensed Cream of Mushroom Soup (Regular *or* 98% Fat Free)**
- **½ cup Campbell's® Condensed Chicken Broth**
- **1 cup shredded Cheddar *or* crumbled blue cheese (about 4 ounces)**

1. Spray the inside of a 6-quart slow cooker with the cooking spray. Layer **one third** of the potatoes and **half** of the onion in the cooker. Repeat the layers. Top with the remaining potatoes.

2. Stir the soup and broth in a small bowl. Pour over the potatoes. Cover and cook on HIGH for 4 to 5 hours or until the potatoes are tender.

3. Top the potatoes with the cheese. Cover and let stand for 5 minutes or until the cheese is melted.

Slow Cooker Western Egg Strata

Makes 12 servings

PREP TIME
15 minutes

COOK TIME
7 hours

Vegetable cooking spray

- **8 slices Pepperidge Farm® White Sandwich Bread, cut into cubes**
- **3 cups frozen diced potatoes (hash browns)**
- **1 pound maple-flavored ham steak, diced**
- **1 large onion, chopped (about 1 cup)**
- **1 large green pepper, chopped (about 1 cup)**
- **2 cups shredded Cheddar cheese (about 8 ounces)**
- **1 can (10¾ ounces) Campbell's® Condensed Cream of Mushroom Soup (Regular *or* 98% Fat Free)**
- **8 eggs**
- **2 cups milk**

1. Spray the inside of a 5-quart slow cooker with the cooking spray. Layer **half** the bread cubes, potatoes, ham, onion, green pepper and cheese in the cooker. Repeat the layers.

2. Beat the soup, eggs and milk in a medium bowl with a fork or whisk. Pour over the bread mixture. Press the bread mixture into the soup mixture to coat.

3. Cover and cook on LOW for 7 to 8 hours or until set.

Kitchen Tip

For a twist, try Monterey Jack or Pepper Jack cheese instead of the Cheddar.

Not Your Gramma's Kugel

Makes 6 servings

PREP TIME
10 minutes

COOK TIME
2 hours

Vegetable cooking spray

- **1 package (12 ounces) *uncooked* medium egg noodles (about 7 cups)**
- **½ cup currants**
- **1 can (10¾ ounces) Campbell's® Condensed Cheddar Cheese Soup**
- **1 cup cottage cheese**
- **¾ cup sugar**
- **1 teaspoon grated orange zest**
- **2 eggs**

1. Spray the inside of a 3½-quart slow cooker with the cooking spray.

2. Cook the noodles according to the package directions until almost tender. Drain and place the noodles in the cooker. Sprinkle with the currants.

3. Beat the soup, cottage cheese, sugar, orange zest and eggs in a medium bowl with a fork. Pour over the noodles and stir to coat.

4. Cover and cook on LOW for 2 to 2½ hours or until set. Serve warm.

Kitchen Tip

This versatile sweet noodle pudding can be served as a dessert, a brunch dish or a side dish alongside barbecued chicken or brisket.

Satisfying Soups

Creamy Chicken Tortilla Soup

Makes 6 servings

PREP TIME
15 minutes

COOK TIME
4 hours 15 minutes

1 cup Pace® Picante Sauce
2 cans (10¾ ounces *each*) Campbell's® Condensed Cream of Chicken Soup
1 pound skinless, boneless chicken breasts, cut into ½-inch pieces
2 cups frozen whole kernel corn
1 can (about 15 ounces) black beans, rinsed and drained
1 soup can water
1 teaspoon ground cumin
4 corn tortillas (6-inch), cut into strips
1 cup shredded Cheddar cheese (about 4 ounces)
⅓ cup chopped fresh cilantro leaves

1. Stir the picante sauce, soup, chicken, corn, beans, water and cumin in a 4-quart slow cooker.

2. Cover and cook on LOW for 4 to 5 hours* or until the chicken is cooked through.

3. Stir the tortillas, cheese and cilantro in the cooker. Cover and cook for 15 minutes. Serve with additional cheese, if desired.

**Or on HIGH for 2 to 2½ hours.*

Chicken & Herb Dumplings

Makes 8 servings

PREP TIME
20 minutes

COOK TIME
7 hours 45 minutes

- **2 pounds skinless, boneless chicken breasts *and/or* thighs, cut into 1-inch pieces**
- **5 medium carrots, cut into 1-inch pieces (about 2½ cups)**
- **4 stalks celery, cut into 1-inch pieces (about 2 cups)**
- **2 cups frozen whole kernel corn**
- **3½ cups Swanson® Chicken Stock**
- **¼ teaspoon ground black pepper**
- **¼ cup all-purpose flour**
- **½ cup water**
- **2 cups all-purpose baking mix**
- **⅔ cup milk**
- **1 tablespoon chopped fresh rosemary leaves *or* 1 teaspoon dried rosemary leaves, crushed**

1. Stir the chicken, carrots, celery, corn, stock and black pepper in a 6-quart slow cooker.

2. Cover and cook on LOW for 7 to 8 hours* or until the chicken is cooked through.

3. Stir the flour and water in a small bowl until the mixture is smooth. Stir the flour mixture in the cooker. Turn the heat to HIGH. Cover and cook for 5 minutes or until the mixture boils and thickens.

4. Stir the baking mix, milk and rosemary in a medium bowl. Drop the batter by rounded tablespoonfuls over the chicken mixture. Tilt the lid to vent and cook on HIGH for 40 minutes or until the dumplings are cooked in the center.

Kitchen Tip

Leaving the lid slightly ajar prevents condensation from dripping onto the dumplings during cooking.

**Or on HIGH for 4 to 5 hours.*

Chicken Asopao with Smoked Ham and Manchego Cheese

Makes 8 servings

PREP TIME
15 minutes

COOK TIME
7 hours 5 minutes

- **4 cups Swanson® Chicken Broth (Regular, Natural Goodness® *or* Certified Organic)**
- **1 teaspoon dried oregano leaves, crushed**
- **1 large onion, chopped (about 1 cup)**
- **1 large green pepper, chopped (about 1 cup)**
- **1 can (about 10 ounces) diced tomatoes with green chilies, undrained**
- **1 pound skinless, boneless chicken thighs, cut into cubes**
- **¾ pound cooked ham, diced**
- **2 cups *uncooked* instant white rice**
- **1 tablespoon drained capers**
- **½ cup grated manchego cheese**

1. Stir the broth, oregano, onion, green pepper, tomatoes with chilies, chicken and ham in a 6-quart slow cooker.

2. Cover and cook on LOW for 7 to 8 hours*.

3. Stir in the rice and capers. Cover and cook for 5 minutes. Sprinkle with the cheese.

**Or on HIGH for 4 to 5 hours.*

Kitchen Tip

If you are unable to find manchego cheese, use Pecorino Romano or Parmesan cheese.

Bacon Potato Chowder

Makes 8 servings

PREP TIME
15 minutes

COOK TIME
3 hours

4 slices bacon, cooked and crumbled

1 large onion, chopped (about 1 cup)

4 cans (10¾ ounces *each*) Campbell's® Condensed Cream of Potato Soup

4 soup cans milk

¼ teaspoon ground black pepper

2 large russet potatoes, cut into ½-inch pieces (about 3 cups)

½ cup chopped fresh chives

2 cups shredded Cheddar cheese (about 8 ounces)

1. Stir the bacon, onion, soup, milk, black pepper, potatoes and **¼ cup** chives in a 6-quart slow cooker.

2. Cover and cook on HIGH for 3 to 4 hours or until the potatoes are tender.

3. Add the cheese and stir until the cheese is melted. Serve with the remaining chives.

Albondigas Soup

Makes 6 servings

PREP TIME
15 minutes

COOK TIME
7 hours

- **4 cups Swanson® Beef Broth (Regular, 50% Less Sodium *or* Certified Organic)***
- **1 jar (11 ounces) Pace® Picante Sauce**
- **1 can (about 14.5 ounces) diced tomatoes**
- **3 cloves garlic, minced**
- **¾ cup *uncooked* regular long-grain white rice**
- ***Mexican Meatballs***
- **3 tablespoons chopped fresh cilantro leaves**

****This recipe is also delicious with Swanson® Chicken Broth (Regular, Natural Goodness® or Certified Organic) instead of the beef broth.***

1. Stir the broth, picante sauce, tomatoes, garlic, rice and *Mexican Meatballs* in a 6-quart slow cooker.

2. Cover and cook on LOW for 7 to 8 hours** or until the rice is tender and the meatballs are cooked through. Sprinkle with the cilantro before serving.

***Or on HIGH for 4 to 5 hours.*

Mexican Meatballs: Mix thoroughly **1 pound** of ground beef, **1** egg, **⅓ cup** cornmeal, **⅓ cup** water, **1 teaspoon** hot pepper sauce and **3 tablespoons** chopped fresh cilantro leaves in a large bowl. Shape the beef mixture firmly into **24** meatballs. Add to the cooker as directed above.

Mexican Black Bean and Beef Soup

Makes 8 servings

- 2 cups water
- 1 jar (16 ounces) Pace® Picante Sauce
- 1 tablespoon chopped fresh cilantro leaves
- 1 teaspoon ground cumin
- 1 large onion, chopped (about 1 cup)
- 1 cup frozen whole kernel corn
- 1 can (about 15 ounces) black beans, rinsed and drained
- 1 pound beef for stew, cut into ½-inch pieces

PREP TIME
10 minutes

COOK TIME
8 hours

1. Mix the water, picante sauce, cilantro, cumin, onion, corn, beans and beef in a 3½- to 6-quart slow cooker.

2. Cover and cook on LOW for 8 to 9 hours* or until the beef is fork-tender.

**Or on HIGH for 4 to 5 hours.*

Slow-Simmered Chicken Rice Soup

Makes 8 servings

PREP TIME
10 minutes

COOK TIME
7 hours 15 minutes

- ½ cup ***uncooked*** wild rice
- ½ cup ***uncooked*** regular long-grain white rice
- 1 tablespoon vegetable oil
- 5¼ cups Swanson® Chicken Broth (Regular, Natural Goodness® ***or*** Certified Organic)
- 2 teaspoons dried thyme leaves, crushed
- ¼ teaspoon crushed red pepper
- 2 stalks celery, coarsely chopped (about 1 cup)
- 1 medium onion, chopped (about ½ cup)
- 1 pound skinless, boneless chicken breasts, cut into cubes
- Sour cream (optional)
- Chopped green onions (optional)

1. Stir the wild rice, white rice and oil in a 3½-quart slow cooker. Cover and cook on HIGH for 15 minutes.

2. Add the broth, thyme, red pepper, celery, onion and chicken to the cooker. Turn the heat to LOW. Cover and cook for 7 to 8 hours* or until the chicken is cooked through.

3. Serve with the sour cream and green onions, if desired.

**Or on HIGH for 4 to 5 hours.*

Kitchen Tip

Speed preparation by substituting 3 cans (4.5 ounces each) Swanson® Premium Chunk Chicken Breast, drained, for the raw chicken.

Barley and Lentil Soup

Makes 8 servings

- **8 cups Swanson® Beef Broth (Regular, 50% Less Sodium *or* Certified Organic)**
- **2 cloves garlic, minced**
- **1 teaspoon dried oregano leaves, crushed**
- **4 large carrots, sliced (about 3 cups)**
- **1 large onion, chopped (about 1 cup)**
- **½ cup *uncooked* dried lentils**
- **½ cup *uncooked* pearl barley**

1. Stir the broth, garlic, oregano, carrots, onion, lentils and barley in a 3½- to 6-quart slow cooker.

2. Cover and cook on LOW for 8 to 9 hours* or until the lentils and barley are tender.

**Or on HIGH for 4 to 5 hours.*

PREP TIME
10 minutes

COOK TIME
8 hours

Yellow Split Pea Soup with Andouille Sausage

Makes 6 servings

PREP TIME
15 minutes

COOK TIME
4 hours

5 cups Swanson® Chicken Broth (Regular, Natural Goodness® *or* Certified Organic)
3 medium carrots, thinly sliced (about 1½ cups)
3 stalks celery, thinly sliced (about 1½ cups)
1 large red onion, finely chopped (about 1 cup)
¼ cup chopped fresh parsley
4 cloves garlic, chopped
1 bay leaf
2 cups dried yellow split peas
6 ounces andouille sausage, diced (about 1½ cups)

1. Stir the broth, carrots, celery, onion, parsley, garlic, bay leaf, split peas and sausage in a 4-quart slow cooker.

2. Cover and cook on HIGH for 4 to 5 hours* or until the vegetables are tender. Remove the bay leaf.

3. Place ⅓ of the broth mixture into a blender or food processor. Cover and blend until almost smooth. Pour the mixture into a 3-quart saucepan. Repeat the blending process twice more with the remaining broth mixture. Cook over medium heat until the mixture is hot and bubbling.

**Or on LOW for 7 to 8 hours.*

Fennel Soup au Gratin

Makes 8 servings

PREP TIME
15 minutes

COOK TIME
5 hours

- **8 cups Swanson® Beef Broth (Regular, 50% Less Sodium *or* Certified Organic)**
- **2 tablespoons dry sherry**
- **2 teaspoons dried thyme leaves, crushed**
- **3 tablespoons butter**
- **1 bulb fennel, sliced (about 4 cups)**
- **2 large onions, sliced (about 4 cups)**
- **8 slices French bread, about ½-inch thick**
- **½ cup shredded Italian blend cheese (about 2 ounces)**

1. Stir the broth, sherry, thyme, butter, fennel and onions in a 5½-quart slow cooker. Cover and cook on HIGH for 5 to 6 hours or until the vegetables are tender.

2. Heat the broiler. Place the bread slices on a baking sheet. Top **each** bread slice with **1 tablespoon** of the cheese. Broil 4 inches from the heat for 1 minute or until the cheese is melted.

3. Divide the soup mixture among **8** serving bowls. Top **each** with **1** cheese toast.

Savory Barley & Tomato Soup

Makes 6 servings

PREP TIME
15 minutes

COOK TIME
6 hours

- **1 can (10¾ ounces) Campbell's® Condensed Golden Mushroom Soup**
- **1 can (10½ ounces) Campbell's® Condensed Chicken Broth**
- **1 can (about 28 ounces) diced tomatoes**
- **2 soup cans water**
- **2 large onions, diced (about 2 cups)**
- **2 cloves garlic, minced**
- **3 large carrots, diced (about 1½ cups)**
- **½ cup *uncooked* pearl barley**
- **1 teaspoon dried Italian seasoning, crushed**
- **2 tablespoons chopped fresh parsley**
- **1 cup grated Parmesan cheese**
- **Croutons (optional)**

1. Stir the soup, broth, tomatoes, water, onions, garlic, carrots, barley and Italian seasoning in a 6-quart slow cooker.

2. Cover and cook on LOW for 6 to 7 hours* or until the barley is tender, stirring once during cooking. Stir in the parsley and cheese. Top with the croutons and additional Parmesan cheese, if desired.

Kitchen Tip

Stir in some Swanson® Chicken Broth or water to adjust the consistency, if desired.

**Or on HIGH for 4 to 5 hours.*

Poblano Corn Chowder with Chicken and Chorizo

Makes 8 servings

PREP TIME
15 minutes

COOK TIME
7 hours

- **4 cups Swanson® Chicken Broth (Regular, Natural Goodness® *or* Certified Organic)**
- **1 tablespoon sugar**
- **2 cans (about 14.5 ounces *each*) cream-style corn**
- **1 large potato, diced (about 2 cups)**
- **2 large poblano chiles, seeded and diced (about 2 cups)**
- **1 package (10 ounces) frozen whole kernel corn, thawed**
- **1 pound skinless, boneless chicken breast *and/or* thighs, cut into cubes**
- **½ pound chorizo sausage, diced**
- **1 cup heavy cream**
- **¼ cup chopped fresh cilantro leaves**

1. Stir the broth, sugar, canned corn, potato, chiles, thawed corn, chicken and sausage in a 6-quart slow cooker.

2. Cover and cook on LOW for 7 to 8 hours* or until the chicken is cooked through. Stir in the cream and cilantro.

**Or on HIGH for 4 to 5 hours.*

Kitchen Tip

To enhance the flavor of the chowder, roast the chiles and thawed frozen corn before adding to the cooker. Place the chiles and thawed corn in a single layer in a roasting pan. Drizzle with 1 tablespoon olive oil. Toss to coat. Bake at 375°F. for 30 minutes.

Persian Split Pea Soup

Makes 8 servings

5 **cups Swanson® Chicken Broth (Regular, Natural Goodness® *or* Certified Organic)**
2 **pounds beef for stew, cut into 2-inch pieces**
3 **leeks, cut into 1-inch pieces**
1 **large onion, chopped (about 1 cup)**
1½ **cups dried yellow split peas**
5 **cloves garlic, minced**
3 **bay leaves**
1 **teaspoon dried oregano leaves, crushed**
2 **teaspoons ground cumin**
½ **cup golden raisins**
2 **tablespoons lemon juice**

1. Stir the broth, beef, leeks, onion, split peas, garlic, bay leaves, oregano, cumin, raisins and lemon juice in a 6-quart slow cooker.

2. Cover and cook on LOW for 7 to 8 hours or until the beef is fork-tender. Remove the bay leaves.

PREP TIME
15 minutes

COOK TIME
7 hours

Kitchen Tip

You can substitute lamb for the beef.

Winter Squash Soup

Makes 8 servings

PREP TIME
20 minutes

COOK TIME
7 hours 10 minutes

- **5¼ cups Swanson® Chicken Broth (Regular, Natural Goodness® *or* Certified Organic)**
- **¼ cup packed brown sugar**
- **2 tablespoons minced fresh ginger root**
- **1 cinnamon stick**
- **1 butternut squash (about 1¾ pounds), peeled, seeded and cut into 1-inch pieces (about 4 cups)**
- **1 large acorn squash, peeled, seeded and cut into 1-inch pieces (about 3½ cups)**
- **1 large sweet onion, coarsely chopped (about 1 cup)**

1. Stir the broth, brown sugar, ginger root, cinnamon stick, squash and onion in a 6-quart slow cooker.

2. Cover and cook on LOW for 7 to 8 hours or until the squash is tender.

3. Remove the cinnamon stick. Place ⅓ of the squash mixture into a blender or food processor. Cover and blend until smooth. Pour the mixture into a 4-quart saucepan. Repeat the blending process twice more with the remaining squash mixture. Cook over medium heat until the mixture is hot.

Creamy Winter Squash Soup: Stir in **½ cup** of half-and-half before reheating the soup in step 3.

Quick Prep Desserts

Chocolate Cappuccino Bread Pudding

Makes 8 servings

PREP TIME
20 minutes

COOK TIME
2 hours

Vegetable cooking spray
1 loaf (24 ounces) Pepperidge Farm® Farmhouse™ Hearty White Bread, cut into cubes (about 15 cups)
4 cups milk
¼ cup heavy cream
6 large eggs
1 tablespoon vanilla extract
1 cup granulated sugar
1 cup packed light brown sugar
¼ cup unsweetened cocoa powder
1 tablespoon instant espresso powder
1 cup semi-sweet chocolate pieces

1. Spray the inside of a 6-quart slow cooker with the cooking spray. Place the bread cubes into the cooker.

2. Beat the milk, cream, eggs and vanilla extract with a fork in a large bowl.

3. Stir the granulated sugar, brown sugar, cocoa powder and espresso powder in a medium bowl. Stir into the milk mixture.

4. Pour the milk mixture over the bread cubes. Stir and press the bread cubes into the milk mixture to coat. Sprinkle with the chocolate pieces.

5. Cover and cook on HIGH for 2 to 3 hours or until set.

Kitchen Tip

Serve warm with whipped cream or vanilla ice cream, and topped with toasted chopped almonds or pecans.

Gingerbread with Dried Cherries

Makes 6 servings

PREP TIME
15 minutes

COOK TIME
2 hours

Vegetable cooking spray
3 cups all-purpose flour
1 teaspoon baking powder
1 teaspoon baking soda
1 teaspoon ground cinnamon
1 teaspoon ground ginger
¼ teaspoon salt
¼ teaspoon allspice
1 cup (2 sticks) butter, softened
½ cup packed brown sugar
4 eggs
¾ cup molasses
1 cup V8® 100% Vegetable Juice
1 cup dried cherries
Whipped cream (optional)

1. Spray a 4-quart slow cooker with the cooking spray.

2. Stir the flour, baking powder, baking soda, cinnamon, ginger, salt and allspice in a medium bowl.

3. Place the butter and brown sugar into a large bowl. Beat with an electric mixer on medium speed until creamy. Beat in the eggs and molasses.

4. Reduce the speed to low. Alternately beat in the flour mixture and the vegetable juice. Stir in the cherries. Pour the batter into the cooker.

5. Cover and cook on HIGH for 2 to 3 hours or until a toothpick inserted in the center comes out with moist crumbs. Spoon the gingerbread into bowls. Top with the whipped cream, if desired.

Tropical Pudding Cake

Makes 8 servings

PREP TIME
15 minutes

COOK TIME
2 hours

STAND TIME
30 minutes

2 cups all-purpose flour
⅔ cup sugar
2 teaspoons baking powder
1 teaspoon ground cinnamon
8 tablespoons butter, melted
1 cup milk
1 can (21 ounces) canned sliced apple
1 can (20 ounces) crushed pineapple, drained
¾ cup toasted walnuts
2 cups packed brown sugar
2 cups V8 Splash® Tropical Blend Juice Drink
2 cups water
Vanilla ice cream (optional)

1. Stir the flour, sugar, baking powder and cinnamon in a large bowl. Stir **half** of the butter and the milk into the flour mixture. Stir the apples, pineapple and walnuts into the batter. Pour into a 4-quart slow cooker.

2. Heat the brown sugar, juice drink, water and remaining butter in a 3-quart saucepan over medium-high heat to a boil. Cook for 2 minutes, stirring often. Pour over the batter in the slow cooker.

3. Cover and cook on HIGH for 2 to 3 hours or until a toothpick inserted in the center comes out with moist crumbs.

4. Turn off the cooker. Uncover and let stand for 30 minutes. Serve with vanilla ice cream, if desired.

Brown Sugar Spice Cake

Makes 8 servings

PREP TIME
10 minutes

COOK TIME
2 hours

Kitchen Tip

This warm, gooey dessert would be great sprinkled with crunchy candied walnuts.

Vegetable cooking spray
1 can (10¾ ounces) Campbell's® Condensed Tomato Soup (Regular *or* Healthy Request®)
½ cup water
2 eggs
1 box (about 18 ounces) spice cake mix
1¼ cups hot water
¾ cup packed brown sugar
1 teaspoon ground cinnamon
Vanilla ice cream

1. Spray the inside of a 4-quart slow cooker with the cooking spray.

2. Combine the soup, water, eggs and cake mix in a medium bowl and mix according to the package directions. Pour the batter into the cooker.

3. Stir the water, brown sugar and cinnamon in a small bowl. Pour over the batter.

4. Cover and cook on HIGH for 2 hours or until a knife inserted in the center comes out clean.

5. Spoon the cake into bowls, spooning the sauce from the bottom of the cooker. Serve warm with the ice cream.

Raisin Cinnamon Bread Pudding

Makes 6 servings

Vegetable cooking spray
10 slices Pepperidge Farm® Raisin Cinnamon Swirl Bread, cut into cubes (about 5 cups)
1 can (14 ounces) sweetened condensed milk
1 cup water
1 teaspoon vanilla extract
4 eggs, beaten
Vanilla ice cream (optional)

1. Spray the inside of a 4½- to 5-quart slow cooker with the cooking spray.

2. Place the bread cubes into the cooker.

3. Beat the milk, water, vanilla extract and eggs with a fork in a medium bowl. Pour over the bread mixture. Stir and press the bread cubes into the milk mixture to coat.

4. Cover and cook on LOW for 2½ to 3 hours or until set. Serve warm with the ice cream, if desired.

PREP TIME
10 minutes

COOK TIME
2 hours 30 minutes

Chocolate Almond Bread Pudding with Dried Cherries

Makes 6 servings

PREP TIME
10 minutes

COOK TIME
2 hours 30 minutes

Vegetable cooking spray
10 slices Pepperidge Farm® White Sandwich Bread, cut into cubes (about 5 cups)
½ cup dried cherries, chopped
½ cup semi-sweet chocolate pieces
1¾ cups milk
½ cup sugar
⅓ cup unsweetened cocoa powder
½ teaspoon almond *or* vanilla extract
4 eggs, beaten
Sweetened whipped cream (optional)
Toasted almonds (optional)

1. Spray the inside of a 4½- to 5-quart slow cooker with the cooking spray.

2. Place the bread cubes into the cooker. Sprinkle with the cherries and chocolate.

3. Beat the milk, sugar, cocoa, extract and eggs in a medium bowl with a fork or whisk. Pour over the bread mixture. Stir and press the bread cubes into the milk mixture to coat.

4. Cover and cook on LOW for 2½ to 3 hours or until set. Serve warm with the whipped cream and almonds, if desired.

Kitchen Tip

This recipe is also delicious with white chocolate chunks instead of the semi-sweet chocolate pieces.

Peach & Berry Cobbler

Makes 6 servings

PREP TIME
5 minutes

COOK TIME
4 hours

Vegetable cooking spray
1 package (16 ounces) frozen peach slices
1 package (16 ounces) frozen mixed berries (strawberries, blueberries *and* raspberries)
1 cup V8 V-Fusion® Peach Mango Juice
1 tablespoon cornstarch
1 teaspoon almond extract
1 package (18.25 ounces) yellow cake mix
1 stick butter (4 ounces), cut into pieces
Confectioners' sugar

1. Spray the inside of a 6-quart slow cooker with the cooking spray. Place the peaches and berries into the cooker.

2. Stir the juice, cornstarch and almond extract in a small bowl. Pour into the cooker.

3. Sprinkle the cake mix over the fruit mixture. Dot with the butter.

4. Layer **8** pieces of paper towel across the top of the cooker. Place the cooker cover on top*.

5. Cook on LOW for 4 to 5 hours** or until the fruit mixture boils and thickens and the topping is cooked through. Sprinkle with the confectioners' sugar.

**The paper towels will absorb any moisture that rises to the top of the cooker.*
***Do not lift the cover on the cooker at all during the first 3 hours of the cook time.*

Harvest Fruit Compote

Makes 10 servings

1 lemon
2 packages (12 ounces ***each***) prunes (about 4 cups)
1 package (7 ounces) mixed dried fruit (about 1½ cups)
1 package (about 6 ounces) dried apricots (about 1½ cups)
½ cup dried cranberries
⅓ cup raisins
4 cups V8 V-Fusion® Pomegranate Blueberry Juice
1 cup white Zinfandel wine
1 teaspoon vanilla extract

PREP TIME
10 minutes

COOK TIME
4 hours

1. Grate **1 teaspoon** zest from the lemon.

2. Stir the prunes, mixed fruit, apricots, cranberries, raisins, juice, wine, lemon zest and vanilla extract in a 6-quart slow cooker.

3. Cover and cook on HIGH for 4 to 5 hours*.

**Or on LOW for 7 to 8 hours.*

Kitchen Tip

The compote can be served warm or cold. Try it warm spooned over vanilla ice cream or pound cake. Try it warm or cold as an accompaniment to roast pork loin.

Triple Chocolate Pudding Cake with Raspberry Sauce

Makes 12 servings

PREP TIME
10 minutes

COOK TIME
6 hours

Vegetable cooking spray
- **1 package (about 18 ounces) chocolate cake mix**
- **1 package (about 3.9 ounces) chocolate instant pudding and pie filling mix**
- **2 cups sour cream**
- **4 eggs**
- **1 cup V8® 100% Vegetable Juice**
- **¾ cup vegetable oil**
- **1 cup semi-sweet chocolate pieces**

Raspberry dessert topping
Whipped cream

1. Spray the inside of a 4-quart slow cooker with the cooking spray.

2. Beat the cake mix, pudding mix, sour cream, eggs, vegetable juice and oil in a large bowl with an electric mixer on medium speed for 2 minutes. Stir in the chocolate pieces. Pour the batter into the cooker.

3. Cover and cook on LOW for 6 to 7 hours or until a knife inserted in the center comes out with moist crumbs. Serve with the raspberry topping and whipped cream.

Kitchen Tip

Use your favorite chocolate cake mix and pudding mix flavor in this recipe: chocolate, devil's food, dark chocolate or chocolate fudge.

Cinnamon Breakfast Bread Pudding

Makes 6 servings

PREP TIME
15 minutes

COOK TIME
4 hours

Vegetable cooking spray
1 loaf (16 ounces) Pepperidge Farm® Raisin Cinnamon Swirl Bread, cut into cubes
4 eggs
3½ cups milk
1 cup *plus* 1 tablespoon packed brown sugar
1 tablespoon vanilla extract
¾ teaspoon ground cinnamon
Maple-flavored syrup

1. Spray the inside of a 4- to 6-quart slow cooker with the cooking spray. Place the bread cubes into the cooker.

2. Beat the eggs, milk, **1 cup** of the brown sugar, vanilla extract and ½ **teaspoon** of the cinnamon with a fork in a large bowl. Pour into the cooker. Stir and press bread cubes into the milk mixture to coat. Sprinkle with the remaining brown sugar and cinnamon.

3. Cover and cook on LOW for 4 to 5 hours* or until set. Serve warm with maple syrup.

**Or on HIGH for 2 to 3 hours.*